A prodigal redeemed can  personal journey captured transparent, authentic, be that speaks to every person God's purpose. Her revealing contextualization serves as a powerful reminder of God's grace and sufficiency even when we walk "the other way." This book elevates and exposes us to the following: we make it not because we perfectly hold on to God but because God perfectly holds on to us. Christine's ministerial trajectory and unbridled success speak to young women who through difficult surroundings discovered that at the end of the day life is not about what we do for God, but rather what God, via the atoning work of Christ, already did for us.

—Rev. Samuel Rodriguez
President, National Hispanic Christian Leadership
Conference (Hispanic Evangelical Association)

Life is unpredictable, but that doesn't mean that our faith in God and His plans for our lives have to be unpredictable. *Prodigal Heart* offers practical and authentic answers to rediscovering the way back to our heavenly Father's arms. Christine D'Clario's transparency touches the heart of humanity with the unchanging truth of God's promises. Let her journey of faith inspire and encourage you as you learn to walk closer with God through every season of your life.

—Sergio De La Mora
Lead Pastor, Cornerstone Church of San Diego
Author, *The Heart Revolution*

Christine D'Clario's account of her journey into the darkness of disappointment and desertion is heartbreaking and yet redemptive. The deep dejection of loss and abandonment she experienced, and the pain it brings, is something we all can relate to. Christine recounts with such honesty and vulnerability the grip grief had on her and helps readers see themselves in her story. We feel the joy of freedom that came as God supernaturally revealed His presence to her and let her know He was always with her even when she felt alone. I highly recommend *Prodigal Heart* to anyone who feels distant or disappointed in God. This book will encourage you in your own relationship with your heavenly Father. Thank you, Christine, for your candor and openness as you share with us your struggles and the overwhelming love God showed you. *Prodigal Heart* is a must-read for those who want to understand their grief and find freedom in God's love.

—LaMar Boschman
Author, *A Heart of Worship* and *Songs From the Other Side*
LaMarBoschman.com

Christine is wise and kind, an important (and beautiful) voice in our generation. *Prodigal Heart* is her story told in such a way that any reader will be moved and changed by her courage and her God. I'm grateful for it.

—Annie F. Downs
Best-Selling Author, *Looking for Lovely* and
Let's All Be Brave

Christine's story is a beautiful picture of the redemptive power of God's love! I am excited for the world to read this great new book, *Prodigal Heart*. My wife, Jodie, and I are grateful to call Christine and her husband, Carlos, friends. I am honored to endorse this offering from Christine and pray that God uses it to bless and encourage those who are searching for the love of the Father!

—Mark Harris
Worship Pastor and Artist-in-Residence, Gateway Church,
Southlake, Texas
Former Member, 4Him

In our world, where social media saturation seems to reign, putting on a happy face often means hiding behind a pretty picture. With *Prodigal Heart* Christine D'Clario breathes fresh life into this world of ours with her honesty and courage. She shares and reveals the authentic and relatable truth of being lost and found, of losing hope and finding strength. From grief to grace, from rebellion to redemption—this book will undoubtedly bring hope and help to many!

—CRYSTAL LEWIS
SINGER-SONGWRITER

Christine D'Clario is known internationally as an anointed psalmist who ushers in the presence of God in an unrivaled way through her worship. Anyone who has ever met her will agree that she is genuinely, passionately in love with Jesus. But when you delve beyond her music into the story of her life, you realize that her journey to the heart of God has been forged in times of great of pain and trial, and the songs she sings are birthed from a real-life encounter with the goodness of a recklessly extravagant heavenly Father. In the pages of *Prodigal Heart* we find the story of her path from brokenness to wholeness, from hurt to healing, and from bitterness to peace. Her life is a testimony of the grace of God, but this book isn't only an autobiography—*Prodigal Heart* is a must-read resource that anyone who has faced opposition, loss, pain, or regret can use to find freedom through Christ and His Word.

—AMY SMITH
SENIOR PASTOR, CITY OF LIFE CHURCH
KISSIMMEE, FLORIDA

Christine's genuine love for Jesus not only resonates through her music; it resounds in her everyday life as well. Her message of restoration and forgiveness is not only powerful but also truly inspiring. This book is now an incredible resource of hope that I will be recommending to many.

—JEFFREY SMITH, PHD
SENIOR PASTOR, CITY OF LIFE CHURCH
KISSIMMEE, FLORIDA

PRODIGAL HEART

CHRISTINE D'CLARIO

CHARISMA
HOUSE

Most CHARISMA HOUSE BOOK GROUP products are available at special quantity discounts for bulk purchase for sales promotions, premiums, fundraising, and educational needs. For details, write Charisma House Book Group, 600 Rinehart Road, Lake Mary, Florida 32746, or telephone (407) 333-0600.

PRODIGAL HEART by Christine D'Clario
Published by Charisma House
Charisma Media/Charisma House Book Group
600 Rinehart Road
Lake Mary, Florida 32746
www.charismahouse.com

Cover concept by: Christine D'Clario
Cover photo by: David Teran Photography
Design Director: Justin Evans

Visit the author's website at www.christinedclario.com/english; see also dclariobook.com.

Library of Congress Cataloging-in-Publication Data:
An application to register this book for cataloging has been submitted to the Library of Congress.
International Standard Book Number: 978-1-62999-172-6
E-book ISBN: 978-1-62999-449-9

This publication is available in Spanish under the title *Corazón pródigo,* copyright © 2016 by Christine D'Clario, published by Casa Creación, a Charisma Media company. All rights reserved.

I dedicate this, my first, book to three
very important people in my life:

To God, my perfect Father, who loves me
and demonstrates it every second that I live.

To the memory of my *papito*, my daddy,
who has already run the race and awaits
me in the arms of the Lord in heaven.

To my mother, Mercedes, who served as
both mother and father, standing up to
fight to give me a better future and teaching
me to love God with everything in me.

∾ CONTENTS ∾

✑ ACKNOWLEDGMENTS ✑

I THANK GOD, MY heavenly Father, who despite what I had become without Him still reached out to me and constantly makes it a point to show me how much He loves me every day. To my Lord and Savior, Jesus Christ, who rescued my heart and taught me that He is the expert in restoring brokenness into something beautiful. To the Holy Spirit, my very best Friend, who always guides me through a good path, one of unconditional love and true friendship.

Thanks go to my husband, Carlos, for being so patient and constant in your love for me even in my worst moments, and for protecting me and always propelling me to be better than I ever imagined I could be. I love you. You are my sunshine.

I am grateful to my mother, Mercedes, and the new dad God gave me, Americo, for loving me unreservedly and putting up with my rebellious days, for embracing me in my repentance and surrender, and for always supporting me in my obedience to the Lord.

I am thankful to my younger siblings, Linda and Jonathan, for not learning from the bad examples I may have given while finding my way but for always being my most faithful cheerers, followers, and intercessors.

Thanks go to my pastors and faith family at Gateway Church in Dallas, Texas, for your constant covering of support, prayer, and brotherhood. Thank you for obeying the Lord enough to provide someone like me with a place to belong.

Finally thanks to all my readers for making the birth of this book worth it. I love you, and you are constantly in my prayers.

❧ FOREWORD ❧

EVERY HEART HAS its Gethsemane—that moment when what is most precious is pressed "to death" beneath the weight of overwhelming circumstance.

Jesus had His moment two thousand years ago in the garden by the same name. There, at the foot of the Mount of Olives, in a grove of olive trees, He wrestled with the weight of His own destiny, pressed in prayer beneath the burden of His Father's overwhelming call to carry the sin of the world to the cross—to the death. There on His knees, when the stress outstripped His strength, His sweat fell "like great drops of blood" (Luke 22:44, MEV)—*that* is pressure. And from that great pressure was squeezed one of the greatest statements of worship in the history of humanity: "Father, if you are willing, take this cup from me; *yet not my will, but yours be done*" (Luke 22:42, NIV, emphasis added).

Out of the pressing came the precious.

Later on the cross Jesus submitted Himself to a crushing so severe that it canceled the sin of the world, disarmed demons, unhinged the gates of hell, and tore heaven open for humanity.

Out of the pressing came the precious.

The word *gethsemane* means "oil press." It was no accident that Jesus chose that olive grove for His final night of prayer. He knew that His mission as the Messiah, the Christ, the anointed One of God was to be the olive from which the oil of God would flow—the blood of salvation.

How can there be oil without pressing? How can there be anointing without a Gethsemane? There cannot be.

The first time I heard Christine sing, I felt the oil flow. She raised her face to the Father, opened her mouth, and as she sang, like the woman with the alabaster jar, the aroma of her anointing filled the room. As Christine worshipped, we all met Jesus. It was as if God stooped low at the sound of His daughter's voice. His presence was there in the room with us.

My friends, that is not *talent*; it is *anointing*.

Our immature, *American Idol* culture doesn't understand the difference. All they see is a gift on fire—platforms and lights and cameras and CDs and *fame*, the gilding of human glory. As a culture we tend to elevate and envy these things. We are jealous for our five minutes of fame. We want our moment of glory, our names to be known. But we rarely consider the cost.

Talent is a gift from God. Each of us has some talent. We did nothing at all to receive it. Our Father knitted it into the fabric of our beings as a gift of grace because He loves us. It is a portion of our inheritance given to us before we even have the wisdom or character to steward it. And like the prodigal son, we often squander what we have been given.

Talent is inborn. Skill is a talent honed by someone who is willing to work. But anointing is different.

I've never seen anointing come without pressing. And the pressing is the problem. So few people are willing to endure it. And fewer still will allow God to speak through it.

Christine's testimony is the story of the Gethsemane of her heart. It is the story of how our hurts can lead to our holiness, how a gracious Father can pour the Water of Life through cracked and broken jars of clay—if only we will stay in His hand. Christine has allowed the Lord to speak through her painful circumstances. And as her Father has spoken, healed, corrected, and directed, those same wounds have become water wells.

Out of the pressing comes the precious.

As you read Christine's story, allow the Father, who loves you, to speak into your story—your Gethsemane moments. Allow the Binder Up of Broken Hearts to show you what He can pour through your pressing. I pray you will find that what the devil has meant for harm in your life the Lord can turn and use for healing. And I pray you would find your feet pointing home again, toward the Father, who loves you—who is waiting for you with open arms and a "prodigal heart."

—ZACH NEESE
WORSHIP PASTOR, GATEWAY CHURCH, SOUTHLAKE, TEXAS
AUTHOR, *HOW TO WORSHIP A KING*

✎ INTRODUCTION ✎

J ESUS OFTEN SPOKE in parables, those simple stories that allow us to understand His work, His purpose, and His kingdom. This book is my attempt to be like Jesus, speaking to you through the story of a prodigal daughter—my own, real-life parable. Journey with me to experience redemption, freedom, hope renewed, and a relationship restored between the Father and His child. Since childhood I've walked through very tough times, repeatedly faced a world filled with pain, and battled with myself through it all. But in the end I found joy in surrendering completely to God the Father, who loves me and restores me.

In his book *The Prodigal God* Timothy Keller defines the word *prodigal* as spending everything in a recklessly extravagant way.[1] In the parable of the prodigal son, found in Luke 15, this is what we see him do with his inheritance. However, we also see reckless extravagance in what God did when He loved us so much that He gave His life on the cross for us. In this book I explore the deeper meanings of Scripture relating to how we can live prodigally for God.

In the pages ahead I share my personal story and processes of restoration. I explain how God rescued me from living a double life of sin while I was a leader in the church. This book is an account of my experiences and the lessons I learned from suffering terrible hardships as a child to growing into prodigally wasting myself and finally being rescued by God, who taught me to still live prodigally but for Him and not myself.

Each chapter includes a detailed description of part of my story, followed by what I have learned from God in my healing process. At the end of each chapter you will find a special directed prayer as well as key scriptures to hold on to through the processes of life and inner healing. These prayers are simply an aid, helping us consider specific things we can ask the Father for when facing similar situations. The prayers are simply a guide for you during your prayer time; feel free to use your own words if it makes you more comfortable. The important thing is to hold on to God through prayer during your journey.

The stories I tell in this book, though I share them from a now-redeemed point of view, are solely based on my recollections of the situations I endured and how they made me feel. While some parts do not reflect my current opinions or perceptions, I have written everything from my perspective—given my physical, mental, and emotional state—at the time. Additionally to share these stories in the most specific, real, yet honoring way, several names, occupations, and places have been changed or omitted.

> You will know the story of a woman who has had to face battles and go through the arduous process of restoration from lost to found, from orphan to adopted, from broken to beautiful, and from hollow to whole.
>
> ———·———

Furthermore every name or pronoun referring to God, Jesus, and the Holy Spirit is capitalized as an act of literary exaltation to Him. On the contrary the word *satan* (which simply means "accuser"[2]) or any other word referring to him is lowercased. He does not deserve honor, and it will never be given on any of my platforms, including this book.

Walk with me through the pages ahead as I give an account of God's work in my life. In this book you will see beyond the artist and leader who takes people into God's presence through worship; you'll see *why* I do what I do. You will know the story of a woman who, as everyone else, has had to face battles and go through the arduous process of restoration from lost to found, from orphan to adopted, from broken to beautiful, and from hollow to whole.

It is my earnest prayer that through these words you receive the revelation of God's fatherhood as well as know your identity as His child—two things that go hand in hand.

Part I

~ THE BEGINNING ~

Chapter 1

∽ THE SETTING ∽

I T WAS A cold February night in 1989 in Yonkers, New York. We lived on Highland Avenue, close to everything we needed, yet we remained inside most of the time. Living in the city meant there were dangers outside our doors that we did not want to encounter. Crime was on the rise in our part of town, especially crimes involving drugs, and some crazy things happened. This, however, was greatly overshadowed by the sight of what lay ahead that day.

We were in the car on our way to a family party. Vibrant music and loud celebration were to be expected—I'm the daughter of an Italian-descending Dominican–Puerto Rican mother—which was a bit of a contrast from the quieter and more put-together gatherings on my father's American-Italian/German-Irish side.

We planned to make a stop before we got to the celebration—a stop I'd been anticipating for many days. I was going to see *him*, as I had a couple of times before. All bundled up and warm, I was enjoying the short car ride to the hospital. There was a common thread in what I had heard from the adults around me: "He's getting better. He'll be back home soon. You'll see!" But this time I was going to see for myself. I could hardly wait to finally witness this deeply desired improvement in my father's health.

I knew he liked to drink—and that alcohol was the cause of his illness. He and my mother had some pretty bad arguments over it, making my awareness inevitable. He even tried rehab a few times. However, just when he'd start to "get better," returning to the comfort and normalcy of home, he would slip back into his old habits, and then the cycle would start over again. I'd been in this place before, much more than a child ever should be. It felt like a weird merry-go-round, but without the fun. This time he'd been away longer than ever. Still, I believed in my tiny heart that he had set out to get better and that he would, just as before. I believed it wholeheartedly.

As I felt my cold cheeks thaw in the car's warm air, thoughts flooded my head—thoughts of love, of hope, of happiness, and not one thought to the contrary. Oh boy! I couldn't wait to wrap my little arms around his neck again. I could feel my lips silently moving, almost mouthing the words I would say to him when our eyes met again. The last time we saw him, he wasn't looking too good. In fact, he was a little skeletal and pale. So this time I was ever so eager to see him in this better state everyone kept talking about.

In my six-year-old mind I imagined I'd probably see him perked up, with that beautiful rose color back in his cheeks and his big emerald-green eyes smiling at me as they had done before he got so sick. After all, the previous time I'd seen him, he did say, "Love you. See ya later, Chi Chi!" Oh, how I loved when he called me that. I always rewarded him for it by replying, "*Papito!*" That is a term of endearment for "daddy" in Spanish, and man, how he loved that word! At the sound of it he always did a squirmy little dance of excitement. And so I'd say it again and again until we would burst out in the most amazing, joyous laughter a father and daughter could share.

Before I knew it, the pictures being painted in my imagination were interrupted by our arrival at the hospital. After our entry my sister and I stayed in the lobby with a family friend while Mom went up to see him first. Last time she did the same, and a few minutes later she came to sneak us up to his room—that hospital didn't allow children to visit patients in their rooms. So I waited, hoping. It took longer than usual, but I waited patiently.

Suddenly the elevator bell dinged, and my mother walked out of the elevator slowly in our direction. Right away I could tell by her facial expression that something was not right. Her red-rimmed eyes struggled to hold tears back. She reached toward us and, her voice trembling from shock, burst out: "I couldn't revive him. He was half dead in my arms. I tried to wake him up. I even threw some cold water in his face, but I couldn't wake him up. I couldn't bring him back." She burst into the saddest and most heartbreaking sobs I had ever heard. My mommy—always the strongest and most joyful woman I knew—was crumbling under a weight I couldn't see and in a way I didn't ever think possible. As she wailed and others tried to comfort her, all I could do was stare, stunned by the truth that she was trying so desperately to say.

Shock overcame me, and time seemed to stand still. Ringing loud and continuous within my mind was: "What? Is she saying what I think she's saying? Maybe she's talking about someone else. Certainly not…" My thoughts paused for a moment as I stared blankly into a scary abyss of uncertainty and disbelief. "Daddy? Wait. Daddy's gone?"

And then there was silence—a long, deep silence, as if my tether to my daddy's heart had been cut suddenly. My *papito* was gone.

EVERYONE HAS A SETTING

Everyone has a setting. It's that moment, place, instance, or set of circumstances that starts it all and sets everything into motion. Every setting places us on a path. The setting—what happens early in our lives—paves the way for the major outcomes in our lives. Every decision within our paths either draws us closer to God or takes us further from Him. My setting comprised New York in the 1980s; a God-fearing, multicultural family background; and grief.

Growing up in a Latin family had its benefits. When my father died, the warmth of loving people often enveloped me like a blanket. There was always someone to play and smile with, always someone I could count on to hold me, especially in such a difficult time of loss. Another part of that setting was church. My mother found Christ years before I was born. She was led to the Lord by my grandparents, the two most loving and faithful Christians I know. Mom fell in love with Jesus from day one. She and my grandparents would bring my sister and me to church weekly, making sure we got involved and learned the Word of God.

We were prayerful, born-again believers. As such there was scripture to be quoted in every situation. Mom made sure of it. Also very often Mom would fill our home with her voice intoning a traditional church hymn or one of her favorite *coritos* (the Spanish word for choruses repeated during worship time in many Hispanic churches). It would soon become a sing-along, as my inclination to music would nudge me to do just that since an early age.

> We must let go of what we've been gripping before we can grab hold of God.

My father seemed to love God, or at least have great fear and reverence for Him. Still I seldom witnessed my dad express devotion to God the way my mother did. He tried going to church with us a few times but wouldn't persevere. Who knows, maybe it was the fact that we went to an all-Hispanic congregation in the Bronx, and he didn't speak any Spanish. Or maybe he wasn't willing to hold on to Jesus as tightly as he held on to his addictions.

One thing that is clear now is because we have only two hands, we must let go of what we've been gripping before we can grab hold of God. Dad had to learn this the hard way, but he sure did learn it. In fact, two days before he passed, he finally let go and invited Jesus into his heart with true repentance. I firmly believe it was not too late. Instead, God's timing with Dad's passing was perfect. He took Dad home to heaven and saved him—and us—from going back through his vicious cycle and ending up lost again, potentially for good. That was one battle over which the enemy sure didn't get to boast victory. God saved Dad and gave us the hope of seeing him again when our lives on earth expire and we go home. Hallelujah!

I was a little girl with a big heart in a big city, with many people to love and be loved by. My setting was filled with as much cultural diversity as flowed through my veins and included loss, pain, and grief. The mixture of these things could lead to one of two paths: edification or destruction. It was from this setting that God traced walkways where I'd have to choose whether to bloom or wither away.

TRAIN UP A CHILD

Many people know the scripture "Train up a child in the way he should go, and when he is old he will not depart from it" (Prov. 22:6, MEV). Whatever is constant in a child's life foreshadows his or her future. It's interesting how children can be so upright, so set in their ways, yet so easily swayed. They're usually quick to answer when asked what they want in life—who they want to be when they grow up, where they want to live, who they want to meet or be friends with—sometimes responding more decidedly than adults do. Yet they seem to be most vulnerable to the enemy's evil plans. In fact, children seem to be at the bull's-eye of these destructive attacks.

There are so many ways children are viciously attacked. Surely you've heard or seen something on the news about a child who is terribly ill, facing injustice, or out on the street, or who has been abused, abducted, or even killed. Here are some eye-opening statistics:

+ One of every two marriages ends in divorce, and many of the divorcing families involve children.[1]

+ Around 20 percent of women and nearly 8 percent of men report having been sexually abused as children. Approximately 25 percent of adults say they were physically abused as children.[2]

+ Nearly one-third of adolescent girls report that
  their first sexual experience was forced.[3]

+ Nearly two million children are in the commer-
  cial sex trade worldwide. An estimated 600,000 to
  800,000 children, women, and men are trafficked
  across international borders each year. Human
  trafficking is a $32 billion industry.[4]

+ According to the World Health Organization
  (WHO), 31,000 children die at the hands of
  adults each year. The majority of those children
  are younger than four years old.[5]

+ Twenty-five to 50 percent of all children report fre-
  quent and severe physical abuse, including being
  kicked, beaten, or tied up by caregivers.[6]

+ WHO estimates that 150 million girls and 73 million boys under age 18 endure forced sexual inter-
  course or violence.[7]

With these statistics it's clear to see that there is an active plan
to tarnish the lives and futures of our children. That's not to men-
tion how much the media is bombarding their minds every day.
If we look closer at the phrase "Train up a child...," in Proverbs
22:6, we can immediately tell that the strategy of the enemy of
our souls is to throw all kinds of wrenches into the wheels of our
little ones. Here's why I think that is. There is an old Spanish
adage that says, "Más sabe el diablo por viejo que por diablo," which
translates as "The devil knows more for his old age than for being
the devil." And I believe it is true.

Let me be clear; I do not give any credit to the devil. Only
God is omnipotent (all-powerful), omnipresent (in all places), and
omniscient (all-knowing). However, likely the kingdom of darkness has learned to identify the telltale signs of greatness in each
of us as a child of God. Moreover, oftentimes the enemy knows

more about our purpose than we do. Of course I am not implying that he is more knowledgeable than Christ—Jesus overcame all powers of evil on the cross (Col. 2:15).

Think about it. The enemy has been witness to the full ancestry of mankind all the way back to Adam and Eve. The kingdom of darkness also has been made privy to God's communion with man, and all those within that kingdom hate it. They've probably cringed at the sound of God's making promises to His people throughout every generation. As with the biblical principle of sowing and reaping, the greatness and blessings due our fore-fathers are passed down to us (Exod. 20:6), as are their curses (Exod. 18:20).

What's important to remember is this: there is greatness in you. God placed it in you before the foundation of the earth was established. As Romans 11:36 specifies, all things—especially us—are "of Him and through Him and to Him." And nothing can be done without Him, as John 15:5 says: "for without Me you can do nothing." We are of God, through God, to God, for God, and nothing without God. And He is great—the greatest, in fact! Therefore be assured that as we were created in His image, He put His greatness in us to enable us to carry out His purpose—which is why we were sent to this world. We can absolutely achieve greatness with Him and absolutely achieve nothing without Him.

The enemy wants nothing more than to destroy our potential. He wants to crush that greatness out of us

> We are of God, through God, to God, for God, and nothing without God.

because it reminds him of our good Father, whom he hates. It seems as if his weapon of choice to hurt the God he so despises is to do everything possible to destroy you and me. Yes, you, God's most precious creation. Considering Proverbs 22:6, it is evident the enemy's strategy is to throw fatal blows at you at an early age. If he can beat your potential out of you as a child, he'll hit you with his full, nasty force. He will do this to make a deep mark that you carry around for the rest of your life and that will potentially cause you to stray from God and His plan, which He thought over you while He created you, as Jeremiah 29:11 says: "For I know the thoughts that I think toward you, says the LORD, thoughts of peace and not of evil, to give you a future and a hope."

WHAT IS YOUR SETTING?

I've always liked stories—telling them, hearing them, reading them. When I was a child in school, I learned the joy of writing them. Teachers taught me literary terms such as *characters, plot, theme, conflict,* and my favorite, *setting.* The latter refers to "the time, place, and circumstances in which something occurs or develops."[8] Furthermore *set* is defined as "to put (something or someone) in a particular place or posture."[9]

The setting of my story is New York in the eighties, a multicultural home with Christ in its center, a loving family, but also much suffering. That was my beginning. What is *your* setting? Have you ever stopped to think about it? Take a look back at your past, at your first few memories in life. What do you see? Where were you? How were you? Maybe you were born in a poor village with not much to eat, or perhaps you were born with a silver spoon filled with wealth and abundance. Maybe you were raised in a nurturing and stable home environment, or maybe you were abused in more ways than you can count. Perhaps you had a parent missing from home, as I did. Maybe sadly you were orphaned but were blessed to be adopted. Maybe you are still searching for a family. Whatever your beginnings were, I know one thing is true: "All things work together for good to those who love God, to those who are called according to His purpose" (Rom. 8:28, MEV, emphasis added).

I know it may be hard to believe that any of the bad things that have happened in your life will ever work for good, but please believe me when I say they will! God has a habit of making *all*—not just some—things work for our good when we love Him. I am living proof of it. In the next few chapters you'll learn of deeper aspects of my journey and how I was able to find the good in the midst of all the bad.

Whatever your setting has been, know that it is indeed a powerful thing. I don't mean it has power in and of itself. Rather, in God's hands it becomes a powerful tool with which He positions you in a place of destiny where you could not have been otherwise. By letting your setting rest in God's hands, you will come to a place of decision and choice, a place of acceptance of God and rejection of sin and the past, but most of all a place of perfection within God's plan for you.

Your setting is nothing but the road you were set upon to run the race of life into the arms of Love. While you will inevitably stumble and crumble along the way, as you persist with hope, placing your hope in our heavenly Father, He will indeed craft your circumstances into the biggest blessings—ones you couldn't have received otherwise. So what is your setting? Have you embraced it yet? Have you allowed it to bring you closer to God? It is my earnest prayer that if you're seeking how to do that, you find it in the pages that follow.

PRAYING THROUGH YOUR SETTING

If you are coming to terms with your setting or embarking on a journey to overcome the past, I invite you to say this prayer:

> *Dear God,*
>
> *I approach Your throne with praise of thanks. God, You are the Giver of life, and I thank You for mine and because I still have one. Also, thank You for my setting—You who see all things, who set me on my path from the beginning. I receive, accept, and embrace it, and I believe that You have a plan and a purpose for it all. I ask that Your hand guide me when I lose my way and that Your voice steady my heart when I cannot see the full picture You hold for my life. Help me be focused on You and not on my circumstances, for You are so much greater than them all. I will walk secure knowing that "all things work together" for my good.*
>
> *In Jesus's name I pray and believe, amen.*

SCRIPTURES TO HOLD ON TO

Man's steps are ordered and ordained by the LORD. How then can a man [fully] understand his way?

—PROVERBS 20:24, AMP

We know that all things work together for good to those who love God, to those who are called according to His purpose.

—ROMANS 8:28, MEV

For I know the thoughts that I think toward you, says the LORD, thoughts of peace and not of evil, to give you a future and a hope.

—JEREMIAH 29:11

Part II

—◆—

∾ GIRL LOST ∾

Chapter 2

∾ LOSS, PAIN, ∾ AND GRIEF

Pain is a kindly, hopeful thing, a certain proof of life, a clear assurance that all is not yet over, that there is still a chance. But if your heart has no pain—well, that may betoken health, as you suppose: but are you certain that it does not mean that your soul is dead?[1]

—A. J. GOSSIP (1873–1954)
SCOTTISH AUTHOR, THEOLOGIAN,
TEACHER, AND CHURCH LEADER

SUNDAY MORNING HAD come. We were driving to church, as we had faithfully done as long as I could remember. Two days had passed since Daddy's funeral—a closed-casket viewing. I never understood why it was called a *viewing* because I could no longer rest my eyes on my daddy's beautiful, brawny face. After his funeral his body was taken away for his requested cremation. I once overheard his and Mom's discussion about it. "I refuse to be eaten by worms," he said, which seemed to be frustrating for her to hear. Yet at the sight of my nosy little head peeking into the room, they eased away from that topic. Of course at that time I didn't know *this* was what they were talking about.

My grandma, his mother, was to lay his ashes to rest near her house, close to the New York–Canada border. Sadly he would be the first to lie in the family's burial ground. Up to that point I hadn't cried as much as one would expect. Perhaps it was because so many people we loved and cherished surrounded us. I certainly loved being around people; I've always found it life-giving to my soul. Even many family members and friends we hadn't seen in a while came to the funeral. Everyone tried his or her best to engulf us with support, sympathy, and affection. At times the joy of seeing them seemed to overshadow my sadness, even if only for a moment.

During the funeral service many people kept my sister and me company the best they could a five- and six-year-old. Funny faces and the occasional tickle attack would send a hint of blissful child's play. The company and apparent fun kept me ever so oblivious to the fact that they were on a mission to keep us newly orphaned kids entertained and perhaps distracted from our crude reality for a while.

Every now and then my gaze would wander and fix itself on the gray suede casket with embossed wavy lines on the surface. Despite what it represented, I thought it was so beautiful. Several times I walked over to it just to feel the soft cover hugging that big box. Behind it the typical funeral home drapes in generic beige were easily superseded by faux candelabra lamps, one on each side of the casket. The many colorful flowers, along one side, seemed so lifeless—or maybe it was just the sadness clouding my eyes.

Atop the sealed coffin was a single picture, one I knew well: our family portrait, taken when I was two or three years old. This was the picture that first made me realize that Daddy and I had the same emerald-olive-green eyes, and that photo sure did them justice. For purposes of the wake it had been covered with a white sheet of paper with a hole cut out to show only *Papito's* handsome face. He was so beautiful. A real looker, if you ask me. Contemplating that picture almost made me forget he was lying inside that pretty gray box.

All these newly carved memories flooded my mind as we rode to church. My mom, a true and faithful servant of God, seemed so calm and poised as we headed out. As was to be expected, words weren't many, but somehow I knew that her unwavering resolve and trust in God were still there. She knew to hold on tight to the Lord, especially then. Suddenly, just when the silence was becoming haunting, my mom gasped, like someone drowning. Then she paused for the longest moment, almost as if questioning whether she should carry on breathing, and then broke down. Her sadness finally had burst through. She began to sob as she had at the hospital after Daddy had passed in her arms. At hearing her heartbreaking sobs, my sister and I followed in kind, wailing in deep sorrow, feeling we had lost everything.

In that moment I felt something I had never felt before. Something began to rise up from the innermost depths of me, from a place that at only six years old I hadn't yet discovered: my soul. It scorched my heart. The feeling was *pain*—not the kind I felt when I'd fall and scrape my knees; that kind could be soothed with Mommy's kiss. This was something else, the worst sensation I'd ever felt. In that moment I became aware that there was an area of me besides my physical body that could hurt as much or even more.

Indeed, my soul—that delicate membrane between body and spirit that contains the mind, will, and emotions—hurt. It hurt so very badly. This pain in my soul stung and stabbed my heart when I realized: "Daddy's gone. He's really gone, and he's never coming back. When we come home from church, he won't be there—not today, not ever." This was my first time experiencing soul pain. It sank deep into my tiny heart and would remain there for years to come.

The culprit of this terrible pain was loss. Realizing I had really lost my daddy made me feel as if I were falling into a sinkhole of despair, losing sight of hope. All I was able to do was scream and cry, so that is what I did. I cried all the way to church. I cried every time someone mentioned him. I cried on our way back home. And I collapsed on my bed when I breathed in his scent still lingering in the room but could not find him there—not then, not ever. The pain was so great I felt I was drowning in it. And so for the first time, I became aware that my soul was wounded.

--- ◆ ---

PAIN AND LIFE GO HAND IN HAND

Unfortunately pain is no stranger to any of us, though it is something we all desperately wish we could avoid. Most of the time when we try to keep away from danger, what we're really trying to avoid is pain. For instance, we don't cross the street when vehicles are oncoming because we know it's dangerous. But our awareness of danger is truly to help us avoid the pain we would feel if we were to be struck.

When we face painful situations, we tend to adopt behaviors and lifestyles that help us alleviate or forget the pain. Some people, whether they know it or not, even morph their bodies and souls to cope with pain. However, I've learned that the best way to deal with it is not to avoid it but to accept it, find its source, and heal from it—which is the tricky part.

The first step to healing from life's painful blows is to accept the truth about what pain really is: a reminder of life. Pain is the evidence that we are still alive, and therefore we can do something about it. Pain is the alarm that warns us when something is wrong so we can address it and remain alive. Think about it: if there were not beating hearts in our chests or breaths of life in our lungs, it would be impossible for us to feel pain. The only time someone stops feeling pain is when he or she is dead. Otherwise, pain is a fact of life.

PAIN: THE HOPE MAKER

A popular saying is "While there is life, there is hope." The Bible in Ecclesiastes 9:4 says, "But for him who is joined to all the living [still alive] there is hope." (MEV). Scripture clearly states that while there's life in us, there is hope. The same way that pain is evidence of life, it is also an assurance of hope. Therefore whenever pain strikes, it is telling us we still have space for hope because we're still here, alive, surviving, and soon to be thriving.

The Bible says, "This hope we have as an anchor of the soul, both sure and steadfast" (Heb. 6:19). This scripture is key to understanding the meaning of *hope*. Hope keeps our souls together when everything else seems to be falling apart. Hope is an anchor that keeps us steady in the storms of life. But hope often comes as a result of painful situations. Hope helps us hang in there through all the pain that is inevitable in life.

Pain was designed to produce hope; hope, in turn, keeps us leveled when in pain. Put simply, pain is evidence of life, and while there is life, there is still hope. Both pain and hope help us grow closer to God.

FACING LOSS AND GRIEF

At one time or another we all face some form of loss and the grief that comes with it. The word *grieve* comes from the Latin *gravāre*, which means "to burden" and is derived ultimately from *gravis*, which means "heavy."[2] Undeniably grief is one of the heaviest burdens a person can carry. Grief is the by-product of loss. Grief is experienced not only when a loved one has died but also with other losses, such as spousal separation or divorce; abortion; and the loss of something else precious, such as a job, a business, health, a home, or even a relationship that left you brokenhearted. What's important to know about grief is while it cannot be avoided, it *can* be overcome.

The best way to overcome grief is to hold on tight to God and His Word. In John 16:33 Christ Himself assured us that we would definitely go through difficulties in life. One of my favorite versions of this scripture is in *The Message*: "I've told you all this so that *trusting me*, you will be unshakable and assured, *deeply at peace.* In this godless world you will continue to experience difficulties. But take heart! I've conquered the world" (emphasis added). Another important scripture that gives us a key to overcoming difficulties is Romans 8:37: "Yet in all these things we are more than conquerors *through* Him who loved us" (emphasis added). Truly the only way to overcome grief is by going through it. As intimidating as that may seem, we can see through these two Bible passages that there is good news. As we trust in Christ, our Overcomer, we can face grief while He weathers the storms of life for and with us. There is hope; it lies within our trust in Jesus Christ!

HEALTHY GRIEVING

If you're grieving right now, you may be losing sight of that hope. While those scriptures are wonderfully life-giving, there are still moments in which it is healthy to hurt and grieve. In those moments following a loss the person who is grieving goes through four stages. Before I discuss those in more detail, I would like to point out some facts about grievers that I've learned through personal experience and many conversations with grief counselors.

First, people who are grieving need the support of others who are willing to accompany them during such a painful process, even if just to listen or provide a hand to hold and a shoulder to cry on. Second, the best way to go through grief is by being aware that it is a natural and painful process that people should face and not avoid. The attitude grievers assume during this process is an important part of overcoming it.

I've found that many grieving people, especially Christians, tend to be one of two extremes: "the positivist under-griever (PUG)" or "the negativist over-griever (NOG)." People need to avoid these extremes to grieve in a healthy, biblical way.

The positivist under-griever (PUG)

I define a positivist under-griever (PUG) as one who projects an overly positive attitude when facing significant loss. People may assume this mind-set to try to either avoid the pain or get through it quickly. They usually hold in their pain, attempting to appear strong.

The PUG attitude gives people the illusion that they can be stronger than they really are or than God intended them to be. Some even attempt to be stronger than Jesus Himself, even though He was among the many in the Bible who wept and mourned (John 11:35).[3] God never intended for us to be strong on our own. We are too fragile to survive under the false notion that we can do it all, be it all, and overcome it all on our own. God's intention for our lives is for us to depend on and find our strength in Him. I do, however, understand that many lean on the PUG attitude as a coping mechanism to try and get over the pain of loss as quickly as possible. Still this approach has two dangerous effects on our souls:

Denial

The Holy Spirit, our Comforter, heals all wounds. However, He ministers and heals in an environment of truth because He *is* the Spirit of truth. John 14:17 says, "the *Spirit of truth*, whom the world cannot receive, because it neither sees Him nor knows Him; but you know Him, for He dwells with you and will be in you" (emphasis added). The world cannot receive the Holy Spirit and His truth because the world *denies* Him. And denial is nothing other than lying—mainly to oneself. Therefore when we push away our painful truths and afflictions and step into denial, we literally begin to live out a lie. The simplest example of this is when we say, "I'm fine," when really we're hurting because of something or someone precious that we've lost. When we admit that something in us is not right and we need God to help us get over it, something happens inside us to help us heal.

Scripture tells us that before Jesus ever healed someone, He would ask the person what he or she wanted healed or done. He did not do it to shame him or her or uncover the person's faulty situation because He is not a condemning or mocking God but one of utmost love and compassion. I believe He asked this to get the person to admit the reality of his situation and need. Had any of the people He healed responded to His question with, "Oh, no, I'm fine," they probably would not have been healed or witnessed a miracle in their lives.

By living in denial, we lie to others and ourselves, which grieves the Holy Spirit—the Spirit of truth—and we become part of the rest of the world that cannot receive Him. What happens with this is we push away our primary ally in the battles of life, the Holy Spirit, the Spirit of truth. He is the only One who can heal us—but again, He does so in an environment of truth. Additionally by maintaining denial (or continuing to live a lie), we become allies to the father of lies, satan, who operates in an environment of lies. As the Bible tells us, one thing is true: we cannot serve two masters (Matt. 6:2). We cannot be in alliance with both God and the devil at the same time. We must renounce one to join with the other. Therefore we must reject satan's lies and embrace the truth so the Holy Spirit can operate freely to heal us.

Soul infection

Have you ever put a bandage on a wound without cleaning it or tending to it? I'm sure if you have, the pain in that wound likely became greater by the minute. That's because that wounded area got infected. The same applies to the soul. When we receive strong emotional blows, such as those caused by great loss, wounds open in our souls. These wounds hurt and often overwhelm us with pain.

In the fast-paced society we live in today, we have become used to instant gratification. Having things such as automobiles, microwaves, the Internet, and many other avenues of acceleration has made us think we can expect the same with the healing of our souls. The truth is any kind of healing takes time and cannot be accelerated further than the time it actually takes. Often we feel a tendency to patch up our souls with quick emotional bandages. Some people overwork to stay busy and try to distract themselves from their pain. Others overindulge in food, television, sports, or entertainment activities as a means to escape. Some even begin to participate in harmful activities, including drug or alcohol abuse. Anything people do to try and cover up the pain a little longer or pull themselves away from dealing with the challenges of grief (often acting as if it never happened) causes their souls to become infected—the other dangerous effect of the PUG attitude. This only prolongs the healing process—and therefore the pain.

I love what CBN published about grief that I believe directly relates to the PUG mentality:

> Grief is a natural, healthy process that enables us to recover from terrible emotional wounds. William Cowper, the English hymn writer, said, "Grief is itself medicine." People may say, "Don't cry; your loved one is in heaven." That may be true, but it's important to deal with the very real pain of loss. We should not feel guilty for grieving because it is a necessary part of God's pathway to healing.[4]

Though our faith must always be anchored in the Word of God, we must never use it to try and escape from the painful, yet necessary, process of grief. Otherwise we risk living in direct contradiction to the Bible's truths about how taking the time to go through mourning is necessary. The Scriptures are clear about balancing out time:

> To everything there is a season,
> A time for every purpose under heaven:
> A time to be born, and a time to die;
> A time to plant, and a time to pluck what is planted;
> A time to kill, and a time to heal;
> A time to break down, and a time to build up;
> A time to weep, and a time to laugh;
> A time to mourn, and a time to dance;
> A time to cast away stones, and a time to gather stones;
> A time to embrace, and a time to refrain from embracing;
> A time to gain, and a time to lose;
> A time to keep, and a time to throw away;

A time to tear, and a time to sew;
A time to keep silence, and a time to speak;
A time to love, and a time to hate;
A time of war, and a time of peace.
                                    —ECCLESIASTES 3:1–8

In so doing, we must know there is a time to grieve. The right way to do this is to be honest and acknowledge our pain, grieve over our losses, and allow God to help us through it all. Our posture should not be one of a PUG. Our hope and help must always come from God (Ps. 121:2). We cannot heal ourselves; only He can heal us.

The negativist over-griever (NOG)

The negativist over-griever (NOG) has an attitude toward grief that persists on the feelings of rage that come with loss, and he remains in that mind-set. I usually see this attitude in people who may serve God but constantly blame Him for their losses. They tend to believe it's all God's fault that they've lost someone or something. While this is a normal part of the grieving process (which I discuss further in the next few pages), the NOG sometimes takes it to extremes, tempting him to live in rebellion toward God.

What I've seen in this type of approach is everything becomes bitterness-ridden for them. They stray from God and His Word, dwelling constantly on the negative implications of their loss. Contrary to the PUG's living in denial, the NOG overly expresses pain. Those who adopt this mentality have a grave tendency to self-inflict more pain with hurtful memories and words, even allowing guilt to penetrate their hearts. It's like rubbing salt in the wound. The worst effect of this state of mind is distance from God accompanied by their desire to remain in their pain. These types of grievers also tend to push everyone good in their lives away to reject any words of hope and support. The only way back to wholeness for NOGs is for them to humbly acknowledge that God is not at fault.

In life we will face troubles; Jesus said so Himself (John 16:33). However, the truth is God will never inflict pain or cause troubles, but He does want us to stay close to Him while we are experiencing them so He can heal and nurture us. We must allow Him to do it through a healthy grieving process.

THE FOUR STAGES OF GRIEF

As part of a healthy grieving process those who are grieving must acknowledge that they are, in fact, hurting and want to heal. A great help is for them to know the four stages of the grieving process—shock, reality, reaction, and recovery—and seek where they stand among them. Following is a description of these stages, according to the Christian Broadcasting Network (CBN).[5]

1. Shock—This stage usually happens during the days and weeks immediately following a shattering loss. The common feelings associated with this stage include a sense of numbness and unreality, as if you're in a bad dream and cannot wake up.

2. Reality—This stage begins when the fact that you've lost something or someone important becomes real to you, taking hold of your mind and soul. This stage comes with the realization that "this really happened." This phase is characterized by the settling in of a deep sorrow, accompanied by weeping and various other forms of emotional release. Often loneliness and depression may occur in this phase.

3. Reaction—Anger is common during this stage. It is often brought on by feelings of abandonment and helplessness. It may be directed toward family,

friends, doctors, the one who died or deserted, or even God. Other typical feelings include lethargy, slowness, apathy, and guilt over perceived failures or personal issues that were unresolved.

4. Recovery—Finally one returns to normalcy but in a gradual and almost unperceived way. This is the time when we adjust to the new life circumstances without the person or thing we've lost. Recovery is one of the most difficult tasks for a person who has experienced major loss, especially if someone dear has departed. Adjusting to the new environment without the loved one is especially hard. This phase is often a long one, and it is best managed when seeking God and allowing Him to show His timing and direction.

I recommend these three steps to better cope with recovery:

1. Grieve—Grief is bitter and filled with sorrow. Yet to heal properly, we must let it run its natural course. Isaiah 53:3 describes Jesus as "a Man of sorrows and acquainted with grief." Denying or repressing pain can lead to emotional problems.

2. Believe—The best way to be comforted in our recovery process is to remember and trust in God's promises, putting our faith in our heavenly Father, believing He knows best and His understanding is perfect. Isaiah 55:9 says, "For as the heavens are higher than the earth, so are My ways higher than your ways, and My thoughts than your thoughts." Furthermore Jeremiah 29:11 assures, "For I know the thoughts that I think toward you, says the LORD, thoughts of peace and not of evil, to give

you a future and a hope." Though we may not see, we must never stop believing.

3. Receive—God loves us, His children. He loves to give us the best and abundant life. That includes comfort when we are suffering. As it is with a physical gift—if you do not extend your hands to receive it, it will not be yours—it is with comfort. It is a gift given through the Holy Spirit, our Comforter. However, we must reach out and accept it to receive it. The best way to do this is through praying and meditating on His Word, finding a place in God's presence, and allowing Him to wrap His arms around us as a loving father would console his hurting child.

As we go through the grieving process, we must remember there is no set time frame for it. Just as when healing physically, each person is different, each grieving process is different, and it requires a different amount of time to heal the soul. We must never assume we can accelerate through these phases. Instead, we must rely upon and hold on to the Holy Spirit as a perfect Comforter to guide us through each step.

CHILDREN AND GRIEF

Since I was only six years old when I lost my father, this subject is close to my heart. This was the first time I had faced true loss. The adults around me at the time weren't fully open with me about the circumstances surrounding my father's death. Now I understand that the reason is they were attempting to safeguard me from pain. However, I still felt the pain of this loss as anyone else, child or adult, would. I know it would have helped tremendously to have someone explain what was going on and what I could have expected.

It is important to know that children may not yet be able to express their feelings or react as an adult would when experiencing the loss of a loved one. Nonetheless they are very much aware of the deep pain that accompanies such a loss, just as an adult would be. Children are still developing their thought processes, their ways of expression, and their communication skills.

If you have or are planning to have children, or you know children, here are a few details I encourage you to take to heart. According to the Children's Grief Education Association, children in varying age groups have different ways to process grief over the loss of a loved one. Infants communicate grief through "sounds of crying, cooing, body language, and physical symptoms such as colic and fretfulness." Additionally they can sense if their caregiver is in distress. Children between three and five years old know what symbolic concepts such as mad, sad, and scared mean and start to express them verbally and tangibly through their five senses: what they can see, touch, hear, taste, and smell. Because they cannot yet understand the future and "never," they expect their loved ones to return.

On the other hand, children six to ten years old may well understand that their loved ones aren't returning. These children especially feel their loss when they compare themselves with other children who still have their loved ones. In this stage of life children develop an interest in biological processes, so they may have a special interest in the natural details of how their loved ones died and what happens to a body after it passes. It is crucial to answer these children's questions in the level of detail they ask. Creative outlets to express their feelings greatly help kids in this age group cope.

Children eleven to thirteen years old are already going through a turbulent time of body changes and the pressures of higher expectations. A death on top of that increases their feelings of insecurity and vulnerability, which may impact their grades at school, as grief is known to affect thinking and learning. Also since they're developing abstract thought, they may consider the spiritual implications of life and death and even question what they believe. It is important to be available to discuss these subjects with the child. Finally teenagers fourteen to eighteen years old who are growing in their independence may feel inclined to hide their feelings, as if to show they are in control of themselves and their environment. Often they would rather talk with peers than adults and are more prone to enter into high-risk behavior after a death.[6]

For the benefit of the grieving children we must keep in mind ways to help them close those painful chapters in their lives to move on. Long-term denial of the death or evasion of a healthy grieving process can be highly detrimental to developing good emotional health and can lead to more severe problems later in life. With regards to funerals the American Academy of Child and Adolescent Psychiatry says:

> A child who is frightened about attending a funeral should not be forced to go; however, honoring or remembering the person in some way, such as lighting a candle, saying a prayer, making a scrapbook, reviewing photographs, or telling a story may be helpful. Children should be allowed to express feelings about their loss and grief in their own way.[7]

More often than not a person
experiencing a big loss just
needs a good listener.

WHAT TO SAY TO SOMEONE WHO IS GRIEVING

Words can make or break us. Proverbs 18:21 says, "The tongue can bring death or life; those who love to talk will reap the consequences" (NLT). When someone is experiencing the loss of a loved one, there are words that can help or hurt. Truly there is no such thing as the perfect thing to say to comfort someone facing great loss or grief, and oftentimes your silent presence can be much better than any word of encouragement you can offer. More often than not a person experiencing a big loss just needs a good listener.[8]

If you do say something, make sure you start your conversation with simple open-ended statements that reflect how sorry you are for the individual's loss. If the time is right for it and the person grieving continues the conversation, make sure you help focus on the good memories of the lost one, allowing the person to express her feelings, and don't overpower her with your opinions or perspectives.

Examples of good things to say are:

+ "I'm sorry your loved one died."

+ "Would you like to talk about it?"

+ "What was he/she like?"

+ "What is the hardest part for you?"

+ "Is there anything I can do to help?"

+ "I'm here to listen if you want to talk, or if you don't want to talk, I'm here if you just want to spend time together."

Though it may seem hard to believe that some of these things have been said, examples of things *not* to say to a person experiencing a significant loss are:

+ "I know just how you feel." (It is impossible for anyone but God to know this.)

+ "Don't cry," or "Lick your wounds and move on," or "You'll get over it," or "Don't think about it." (A statement such as these creates pressure to hurry

*   "It will be OK," or "Be strong." (In that moment
    it is *not* OK, and that person is *not* feeling strong.
    On the contrary it's painful—and that's OK.)

*   "You are better off without him," or "You should
    feel (proud, relieved, happy, sad, and so on)."
    (Never tell a person what she should feel. God
    does not force Himself upon our hearts and feel-
    ings; therefore we should not force our opinions on
    others either.)

*   "Tears won't bring her back." (The tears are not to
    bring the lost one back but for healing. When they
    come, they should not be suppressed. As a wound
    heals through festering, so does the soul through
    grieving.)

*   "If only you had _____, maybe this wouldn't
    have happened." (This statement sets the person
    up for failure. We cannot go back in time and
    undo our wrongs. Therefore we have no business
    bringing up guilt to someone already hurting.)

> As a wound heals through festering,
> so does the soul through grieving.

*   "It's your fault." (These words are a key that opens
    a door to the spirit of condemnation and can
    mean the loss of the person already grieving. We
    must follow the example of Romans 8:1: "There is
    therefore now no condemnation to those who are
    in Christ Jesus, who do not walk according to the
    flesh, but according to the Spirit.")

One way or the other our words carry weight. The Scriptures have a few things to say about being too quick to speak: "Wise people treasure knowledge, but the babbling of a fool invites disaster" (Prov. 10:14, NLT). Later in that chapter Solomon is more direct: "Too much talk leads to sin. Be sensible and keep your mouth shut" (Prov. 10:19, NLT). However, it is a biblical command for us to be willing to help those grieving carry their burdens: "Bear one another's burdens, and so fulfill the law of Christ" (Gal. 6:2, MEV). The best way to follow Scripture when helping grievers—children and adults alike—is to be there and make yourself available to help carry their burdens, doing so with patience and in silence unless asked otherwise.

Grieving is a natural response when we experience loss, pain, and suffering. Our God is well acquainted with grief. If you are facing a tough loss, know that He wants you to go through the grieving process in a healthy way. Remember to grieve, believe, and receive. Don't deny your pain, and don't lose hope in the midst of your heartache. Trust your heavenly Father, knowing that He is good and that He knows best. Remember, God longs to walk with you during times of sadness. He wants to comfort you when you're suffering. All you have to do is reach out and receive His love.

Pray Through Loss, Pain, and Grief

Most likely you have experienced pain over loss in your life. If not, I guarantee you will at some point. If you've been trying to overcome the hurt that comes with grief, I invite you to pray this prayer:

> *Dear Holy Spirit, my Comforter,*
>
> *I am drawing near and reaching out to You in this time of pain. I am hurting and at times feel overwhelmed. Be my strength and my guide through this process. Help me feel You holding my hand and embracing me as I grieve my losses. Help me stay connected to You and focused on Your Word and not my pain. Help me accept the things I cannot change and be fortified in soul and spirit to heal properly. Today I accept and acknowledge Your sovereignty, and I surrender to Your will and choose to follow Your timing and not mine. Today I embrace the truth that You are here with me and will never leave me or forsake me. I trust You. Your loving hand will heal me and make me whole again. Thank You for that, Lord.*
>
> *In Jesus's name I pray and believe, amen.*

Scriptures to Hold On To

If your heart is broken, you'll find God right there; if you're kicked in the gut, he'll help you catch your breath.
—Psalm 34:18, The Message

All praise to God, the Father of our Lord Jesus Christ. God is our merciful Father and the source of all comfort. He comforts us in all our troubles so that we can comfort others. When they are troubled, we will be able to give them the same comfort God has given us.
—2 Corinthians 1:3–4, nlt

Chapter 3

❧ REJECTION ❧

Not until the work in hand has failed and we are despised and rejected shall we begin to discern the intent of our heart.[1]

—WATCHMAN NEE (1903–1972)
CHINESE AUTHOR AND
PERSECUTED CHURCH LEADER

TIME WENT BY, and my eyes seemed dried up. Soon my mom met someone and fell in love again. The pain I thought had subsided crept back up the day she announced she was going to get remarried. That burning sting engulfed my heart's core again. "Did that mean I had to call him 'Dad'?" I wasn't ready for someone new. I still wanted my daddy back, although I knew that was impossible. But who was I to tell an adult, especially my mother, what to do?

Shortly after breaking the news to us kids, they were married. Later they had my baby brother. He was the heart's desire of any big sister. Mom's pregnancy and the birth of my brother brought back a hope I had been struggling to find again. I even had a dream about him before he was born. I saw his ash-blond hair and big hazel eyes before they were fully formed. When he arrived, I remember gazing upon him, thinking, "He's so beautiful…and so mine."

The first few weeks after his birth my sister and I showered our brother with love every day. We instinctively protected him, as any big sisters would. We ran to him whenever he cried, eager to fulfill his every need. Yet as the days progressed, something began to slowly surface in me—something that seemed to have fallen asleep with all the excitement of a new baby in our home. Even though this precious child was everything I ever wanted in a second sibling, his being there started to become painful to me. I began to remember that my daddy wasn't there. The longing in my heart for his embrace or for him to be part of my big-sister excitement began to intensify. My sorrow had awoken again, replacing every smile with lip quivers.

Watching my mom and stepdad, I began to feel the whirlwind a parent goes through with the arrival of a little one. I felt the effects of the great adjustment, the lack of sleep, the moods, and the forgetfulness that comes when a new parent hyper-focuses on a newborn. It hurt to feel forgotten because everyone's attention now rested on this new, little king of hearts. As I was still grief-stricken, my joy often shifted to sorrow when I looked at my baby brother. His birth began to mean more than a sister's dream; in my mind it also meant my dad could well be forgotten forever. Somehow I thought the little one's arrival had obliterated my father from my mother's heart.

I'd already lost my daddy, but losing sight of his memory was terrifying. It was like losing him all over again.

> My sorrow had awoken again, replacing every smile with lip quivers.

With every effort to keep him alive in my mind, I became desperate. As one who is drowning gasps for breath, I grasped every memory to hold on to him. I'd string thoughts together, focusing on the sound of his deep voice, the warmth of his tattooed arms, the way the breeze blew his hair and how it would smoothly fall back into place, the way he looked over his shoulder when he was driving just to wink at me, and the amazing view I had from atop that very shoulder whenever he carried me. It became my mission to keep him beating in my heart because I felt that everyone else was forgetting. In reality it was also an attempt to save myself because I thought if he was no longer in the front row of everyone's thoughts, then neither was I. After all, I *was* half him.

I felt helpless and as if I'd drift away along with the memories of him. So I began to steer clear of distractions from my new mission, one of which was my baby brother.

A few months after my brother was born, another blow hit that tore at my heart and rendered it nearly beatless. My mother and stepfather had decided to move us to a new land, Puerto Rico, where he was born. It was a few hours' ride by plane. Yes, my heart did melt at my stepfather's tales of an eternal summer where I could play on hills with trees from which I could pluck fruit to eat on the spot, surrounded by marvelous Caribbean beaches and all the delicious food and the festive culture that I loved. But moving there also meant I would be taken away from everything and everyone I knew and held dear. That's what hurt. Still my intrigue became excitement as the move grew near.

When the day we were to leave arrived, I took one last look back at our little city apartment, now emptied out by the movers. I could picture the way it was before Daddy fell very ill. I could almost hear his guitar strumming in the other room, smell his famous eggplant Parmesan, and hear his deep voice with an Italian-New York accent. Faced with the hard truth that he was gone and I was too little to resist leaving, I dragged my wounded soul out the door. Hopeless, I had no choice but to let pain cut right through me. In that moment I felt loss strike me again, opening the wounds that had slowly begun to heal.

A few days after we moved to Puerto Rico, we began attending school, which was already in session. In New York I loved school. There was so much to learn and so many kids who, like me, had a mixed background, so they understood me when I talked about my Anglo dad and Latina mom. I was surprised that I was the only one in my new class with such a mixed background. I was immediately labeled *la gringa* (slang for Yankee or North American foreigner) since my Spanish was not in tip-top shape, and my blonde hair, fair skin, and green eyes gave me away. I struggled with culture shock. I struggled with getting up to date with schoolwork in a different school system. I struggled with being accepted. I struggled with rejection. I couldn't fit in no matter how hard I tried.

I've always been a quick learner, so as time went by, I began to adjust and get into a new rhythm. A few of the children in my new stepfamily went to the same school as I did, so we spent much time together. Like every child many had a tendency to bring up who they thought I really was whenever there was opportunity. There were occasions when my new extended family would get together, as any good Puerto Rican family would, to celebrate family festivities. We were together every Christmas and New Year's Eve and for every family wedding, birthday, and *quinceañera* (a Hispanic tradition to celebrate a woman's coming of age at fifteen years old). These were times I both loved and dreaded. I loved them because I got to be surrounded by people I held dear, as in New York. But I dreaded them because every time a cousin or extended family member would meet me for the first time, the other kids would introduce me in a way that was hurtful, even if that was not their intention. Their introductions often went something like this: "This is Christine. She's my cousin. But she's not my *real* cousin." And usually the other party would follow with, "What do you mean?" The answer: "Well, my uncle is married to her mom, but he's not her real dad. Her father died because…he drank too much."

I know now that these kids likely meant well, yet their words dug into a pain I was struggling to appease. Just when I would start to forget how much it hurt, there was a reminder. No matter what I did, I kept finding myself back at that moment of loss. I felt as if I was being sucked into a swirl of sorrow that simply wouldn't let go. The repetition of these introductions soon became a part of me. I came to believe that this was who I was: Christine, the orphan child of an alcoholic father, who didn't quite belong.

Rejection seemed an everyday thing. As I grew a little older

and hit my preteen years, I went through what I call an ugly duckling phase. My hair, though blonde, is where I carry my Afro-
Caribbean curls that often seemed as if they were being paid to
stay frizzy in the hot, humid, tropical air. I'm fair-skinned, so
being out in the sun all day—which was inevitable in this beautiful isle of enchantment—made me turn red. My German-Irish
long and slim body structure gave me the appearance of a stick
figure. And my teeth...oh, my teeth were deformed. Our dentist
told my mother once that I just "had too many teeth for such a
small mouth," which caused me to be unable to close my mouth
as any normal person would. Whenever I tried hiding my hideous
teeth, it looked as if I were making a funny face, but I was feeling
far from funny.

As I grew and changed into this ugly duckling, my peers at
school soon caught on, and I began to go through a season of
being bullied. A few kids pushed me around physically and emotionally. They constantly called me names—picking on many of
my features—that included *la garza*, meaning "the heron," because
of my skinny legs; *el comején*, what they said was a termite nest,
similar to an Afro; *la coneja*, meaning "the rabbit," because of my
protuberant teeth; and *la jirafa*, or "the giraffe," because of my
very long neck. One time a kid at school ran up to me and called
me just plain ugly to my face, then ran away laughing with his
bully accomplices.

I couldn't bear all the unprovoked humiliation. Yet I swallowed
it all, kept it all inside. I felt that I couldn't tell anyone who would
understand. Daddy would have understood. Being cut from the
same cloth, he always seemed to understand me perfectly. But he
was no longer an option. Trying to talk heart to heart with my
stepfather was out of the question. I didn't yet accept him, despite
all he had done to try and win me over, but saw him as someone
who came to take my daddy's place. Mom was usually busy,
rushing home from work to cook, care for the baby, clean, and
prepare us for school the next day or for church several evenings a

week. I didn't want to bother her or add anything to her full plate. My sister, I felt, didn't understand because she blended in perfectly with her beautiful, straight, brunette hair; dark brown eyes; and slightly sun-kissed skin. Furthermore I was the big sister; my thinking was that it was *I* who was to take care of her, not the other way around.

I felt I had no one. My self-esteem shattered and dragged me way down. I became a loner, so I focused on music. At an early age I discovered my love for singing and playing instruments. I listened to music every waking moment. I could become lost in a song so easily. It was common to hear my mom shout from the other room, *"Bájalo!"* ("Turn it down!") because I'd gotten carried away with the volume. As a little girl I began performing songs at church. The first time I was given a microphone and heard my voice amplified, I felt a rush that I hadn't gotten with anything else. Singing became my passion. Music became my friend. Music wouldn't ever judge me, call me names, or reject me. In fact, so many songs spoke of what was on my heart that it was as if I had written them myself.

I dove deeper into this newfound passion for music and let it pull me in whatever direction it would take me in. In my safe zone—in my room, sitting or lying in front of my radio, surrounded by a bunch of cassette tapes (yes, I used to listen to cassettes; then CDs were something of the future)—I felt I could escape, run away in my mind and heart to a place with no loss or rejection. I was free when I dove into a song. I was free when I sang a song. Even when others were watching, I was free from their scrutiny as long as I kept uttering melodies. It was during this time that I decided to cultivate my talents. I would make sure I'd fit in by way of my musical abilities, if not for anything else. I was content to be accepted through music itself—and indeed I was.

———————◆———————

FROM REJECT TO RESET

I know rejection. It was a constant reality for me for many years from childhood. During that time I learned what it felt like, how it hurt, and how to use defense mechanisms to cope with it. It's not an easy companion to live with since it continually nags and harasses your every thought with whispers of not belonging, being disliked, and being unaccepted. I can very well tell you what rejection is all about. Yet all those years I did not have a clue about how to heal from the rejection I encountered. I didn't even think it was possible to mend the chasm in me due to rejection. I considered myself permanently labeled "rejected and unwanted."

After I met God—truly met Him in a miraculous encounter with redemption (I explain this in more detail in a later chapter)—much later in my restoration journey, I realized rejection was a big issue in my life and an area where I needed to heal. I had to go from reject to reset and start fresh, with a clean slate, accepting God's truth in my life. Much of what I have learned about healing from rejection came from listening to my pastor, Robert Morris of Gateway Church, teach on the subject. Most of the truths I'm including in the next several paragraphs come from what God has taught him.

THE ROOTS OF REJECTION

Pastor Robert in a sermon said something about rejection that shook me: "When we feel rejection, we feel as if there [is] something wrong with us. Here's why. It's because there *is* something wrong with us; it's called a *sin nature*."[2] Faced with this spiritual fact, I finally understood why so many people suffer from rejection issues. It's because we are, in fact, born rejected and separated from God because of the sin nature with which we are born. No wonder we long for acceptance. That need for acceptance really comes from our spirits' yearning to get past the barrier of sin into the acceptance of a Holy God and Father.

Scripture is specific about our sin being the cause of our

rejection and separation from God. For deeper understanding I prefer the Amplified Bible version of 1 Samuel 15:23: "For rebellion is as [serious as] the sin of divination (fortune-telling), and disobedience is as [serious as] false religion and idolatry. Because you have rejected the word of the LORD, He also has rejected you as king." Also, in Hosea 4:6 God affirms, "My people are destroyed for lack of knowledge [of My law, where I reveal My will]. Because you [the priestly nation] have rejected knowledge, I will also reject you from being My priest. Since you have forgotten the law of your God, I will also forget your children" (AMP).

Clearly God's rejection comes as a direct effect of humanity's rejection of God, His Word, and His will. Additionally God cannot intermingle with sin. He is automatically separated from it due to His perfect holiness and purity (Hab. 1:13). Even Jesus Himself experienced rejection and separation from God due to bearing all our sins on the cross (Matt. 27:46).

The only cure for the wounds of rejection is to gain God's acceptance. The good news is God wants to accept us. He wants to restore our separation from Him. That is why He sent His Son to give His life on the cross for us. Christ became sin and took on rejection so we could be accepted. We can be accepted back into God through our acceptance of Jesus's sacrifice for us. Hallelujah! When we receive God by accepting the blood of Jesus Christ—the only way to the Father (John 14:6)—God automatically accepts us.

SURRENDERING YOUR REJECTION

It is important to know that simply by our accepting Christ as our Savior, God accepts us. However, this act alone will not necessarily heal our issues with rejection. There is more to it. There must be a surrender and a conscious acknowledgment that we need Him. That's the tricky part, I've learned.

People who suffer from rejection develop a series of defense mechanisms to help them cope with the effects of rejection. Many become master manipulators, deflecting attention to keep people's focus on someone else's flaws instead of their own. Others hide behind a facade of overconfidence. Oftentimes it seems people with major rejection issues are the most confident. A telltale sign of rejection-driven, false confidence is people's need to continually brag or show off what they have, do, or achieve. This is nothing more than their need to feed off of the extra validation to deflect rejection.

The vast majority of people who struggle with feelings of rejection develop a strong sense of pride, even a delirium of superiority. This pride acts as a wall that pushes out anything and anyone that could cause them to feel rejected. Pride also pushes them to lash out and demean others through their words and actions. As I've heard Pastor Robert say on several occasions, "Hurt people hurt people, offended people offend people," and so on. This cycle gains strength and cripples relationships, which pushes people away even more.

Rejection fortifies pride, which caused man's fall into sin and created the separation from God originally. However, we are saved and empowered by grace, our ever-so-undeserved favor. We cannot win grace; it's free to those who humbly accept the Lord. Of course pride doesn't mix with grace because pride tells us we deserve, or are entitled to, what we need. Pastor Robert said the only cure for rejection is to be accepted by God, and the only way you'll be accepted by God is by being confronted with the truth that you *need* God.[3] Therefore if we want to truly be set free from the strongholds of rejection, we must lay down our pride at the cross. When we humble ourselves and confess that we need God and amount to nothing without Him (John 15:5), we can be truly set free from the burdens of rejection. God knows everything we've done, including everything we've forgotten we've done, as well as everything that has been done to us. Still He loves us. He loves us so much that He died for us. He will redeem and heal everything you lay down at the cross—including your life. Surrender is the key.

PRAYING THROUGH REJECTION

If you're like me, not only have you experienced rejection, but also you've likely been badly wounded by it. If you've read this chapter and realize you need to let go of your rejection, I invite you to say this prayer:

> *Dear God,*
>
> *I come close to Your throne in surrender, confessing that I need You. I am nothing without You. I see now that I have been focused on rejection far too long, and today I choose to fix my eyes on You. I speak, believe, and choose to walk in the truth that I am accepted by You, God, through the blood of Jesus Christ shed on the cross for me. I lay down my life, my pride, and my past, present, and future at the foot of that cross. I am not rejected, forgotten, or unwanted. I am accepted, remembered, and wanted by You, the One who matters. Please heal me and guide me forward, never to return to that place of rejection.*
>
> *In Jesus's name I pray and believe, amen.*

SCRIPTURES TO HOLD ON TO

What then shall we say to these things? If God is for us, who can be against us?
—ROMANS 8:31, MEV

Even if my father and mother abandon me, the LORD will hold me close.
—PSALM 27:10, NLT

Just as He chose us in Him before the foundation of the world, that we should be holy and without blame before Him in love, having predestined us to adoption as sons by Jesus Christ to Himself, according to the good pleasure of His will, to the praise of the glory of His grace, by which He made us accepted in the Beloved.
—EPHESIANS 1:4–6

Chapter 4

✂ FEAR AND DOUBT ✂

Worry is a cycle of inefficient thoughts whirling around a center of fear.[1]

—CORRIE TEN BOOM (1892–1983)
DUTCH HOLOCAUST SURVIVOR
AND PUBLIC SPEAKER

A FEW YEARS WENT by. Although I was well-adjusted to living in Puerto Rico, I still missed New York. Yet I'd become content, no, resigned to where I was. Every time I would see an airplane flying over our area, I'd play with my sister and shout, "Wait for me! Wait for me!" Despite my apparently innocent joking, I meant it every time. My soul cried, "Wait for me, and please take me back." That is where I wanted to go, back. I wanted to return to where I felt I belonged, with all my family gathered together, enjoying all four seasons again. I wanted to go back to seeing Daddy again. It still hurt that this was impossible. I would've easily traded a full life in the vast green tropics with perpetual summer for going back to the way things were when Daddy was alive, even if for only a day.

Whereas late childhood was cruel to my physical appearance, adolescence was a kinder stage. After three years of wearing braces to fix the debacle of my protruding teeth, the battle was won. The braces came off. I savored that day and will always remember it as one of the best days of my life. Sliding the tip of my tongue along the straightened, smooth surface of my front teeth was a dream that had finally come true. To this day I do it from time to time and can't help but smile inside, giddy in my relief, just as I was the day my braces were taken off. I thought, "I can finally smile freely without looking like a freak." Soon after the wires came out of my mouth, my dear mother bought me beauty tools: a blow dryer and curling and flat irons. I could almost hear angels sing when I opened the first box! This meant I could finally do something about this frizz ball on my head. I could finally *fit in*.

I mastered my new smile, hair, and makeup in no time. Soon my body began to change. That big-haired, skinny, rickety girl was blooming into a beautiful woman, at least according to those around me. Soon all that rejection started diminishing too. Where once my tall, slim, Euro features were the object of bullying, they now set me apart from the rest. Now I was experiencing something I had craved my entire life: attention. I was no longer the weird girl, but many of my peers referred to me as "exotic." I had never known what it was like for someone to have a crush on me until now. Receiving flowers on Valentine's Day at school was something that had happened only to the other girls— until now. A couple of modeling agencies even approached me, which I thought was crazy, given that I was the ugly duckling up until less than a year before. And I'm not going to lie; I loved this newfound attention. I loved the feeling inside when I'd pass by a cute guy and his head would turn in my direction. This kind of response was always an impossibility, a dream to me—until now.

I entered gracefully into womanhood. Yet despite the rapid whirlwind of apparent overnight acceptance, I missed my father terribly, especially when it came to needing someone to talk to about boys. On the inside I was still that little girl, marked by pain and loss, grieving.

I turned sixteen, and the crown of my adolescence had arrived. I had experienced puberty, and I wore my big girl shoes well. I was quite active in the church I grew up attending, singing at every possible church activity and special event. I was in every choir and ensemble, becoming the go-to girl when the band needed someone to harmonize or sing a solo. The more I sang, the better I felt about myself, especially when others showered me with praise and affirmation. My confidence began to build, eventually towering high. I felt as if I could finally take on the world; all I needed was a microphone and a soundtrack.

Once in a while our church invited a special guest to take part in an event or crusade. At one of those events a fiery preacher spoke. Before the sermon he introduced the church to his son who had accompanied him. I remember looking at him, dazzled by his good looks, but quickly snapping out of it. After all, I wasn't used to being the center of attention when it came to guys. Inside I was still that odd, little reject, regardless of how my teenage hormones had worked in my favor.

At the end of the night my sister, cousins, girlfriends, and I gathered for typical after-church mingling. Hellos and hugs flowed left and right. But this time I felt someone was looking at me. Out of the corner of my eye I saw a guy slowly walking our way. It was the preacher's son. His light brown hair and big blue eyes became more apparent as he got closer. He was slim, tall, and athletic—all things I had written in my diary on my "ideal guy" page. And he was a Christian! My mom always said the number one quality I should look for in a guy is that he knows and serves the Lord.

Thoughts flooded my mind: "What? He's walking over here...?" I immediately doubted: "No. He's probably walking over to meet my sister or my cousins, even my friends, but not me. Certainly not me." After all, my sister is gorgeous. She has silky smooth dark hair; dark, piercing eyes; light caramel skin; and a smile that takes my breath away. She would definitely be the one to come say hi to, I thought. Or perhaps his focus was on one of my cousins, with their sun-kissed complexions, long hair, and curvy bodies that made guys drool. They were stunning beauties. While I was getting acquainted with not being the ugly girl in the group, I was still different—the only one with lighter hair and huge green eyes, usually also the tallest in the group.

A monologue ran through my mind as the preacher's son (whom I'll call Romeo) approached. When he finally got to where we stood, he looked straight at me and said, "Hello!" I was dumbfounded. My face felt warmer as I looked around to see if he was really talking to me. "My name is Romeo. What's yours?" he said. I managed a normal greeting, replying, "Hi. I'm Christine." We started talking. He said he noticed me from across the church and needed to come say hi. Later that night, after we laughed and discovered we had some common interests, he asked for my number. Of course I gave it to him. There was a twinkle in my eye, a flutter in my belly, and a little spark of hope in my heart. For the first time, I'd met a guy who looked an awful lot like the guy of my dreams—and he liked me!

After that night I waited patiently for a call. Days turned into weeks, which became months, and no call came from dreamy Romeo. Doubt reared its ugly head again. I thought: "Of course that guy wasn't going to be interested in me. Me? C'mon. Who do I think I am? I'm not the girl guys fall in love with. I'm just a silly dreamer. What a dumb thought."

Several months later another special event was held at church. Romeo's father returned to preach. And again, there was Romeo, his father's faithful companion. As soon as the last amen was uttered from the altar, he rushed over to me like a dog hiding its tail. I thought, "Let's see what excuse this one cooked up." He said he hadn't stopped thinking of me. "Yeah, right," I thought as I fought the temptation to say it aloud. He proceeded to say he lost my number. He had put the paper my number was on in his pants pocket but had forgotten to take it out before putting them in the washing machine. His charm and story were convincing. He made me laugh as he explained the details. So when he asked for my number again, my melted heart pushed my hands to write it down for him once again. This time he did call. And after that he called many more times, until we began chatting for hours every day. We got to know each other's hearts well and fell in love.

Romeo asked me to be his girlfriend. I quickly said yes. I was madly in love. Truth be told, I was as fearful as I was in love. I had resolved to not get hurt again. I feared that he could one day leave me or hurt me the way so many other people had done throughout my life. I feared I wasn't good enough for him. This fear drove me to become determined to do everything in my power to avoid the manifestation of my fear. I was going to be the best girlfriend in the world, so I devoted myself to being everything he wanted and more.

Soon I made compromises to stay in his good graces, avoid his discomfort, and make sure he was always happy with me. His opinions, tastes, and preferences became mine. If he disagreed with anything I said or did, it would never happen again. When we were dating, there came a point where if he had said, "Jump," I would've instantly replied, "How high, my love?" God was no longer in the center. Now Romeo was my center and my all. I was going to make sure he would be mine forever...or so I thought.

THE DIFFERENCE BETWEEN FEAR AND DOUBT

Often *fear* and *doubt* are considered synonyms, but nothing could be further from the truth. While the two are autonomous, they usually go hand in hand. I see fear and doubt as siblings—they come from the same place but are not the same thing. *Fear* is "a distressing emotion aroused by impending danger, evil, pain, etc.," whether the threat is real or imagined.[2] *Doubt*, on the other hand, is "to be uncertain about...to distrust...consider questionable...hesitate to believe; a feeling of uncertainty, distrust."[3] One thing is for sure: one usually provokes the other. I, for one, thought they were one and the same; when I felt one, I felt the other. Whether I feared or doubted, the end game was the same: to avoid pain.

THE POWER OF FEAR

Fear is a mystery. It can take something tiny and insignificant and blow it up into unreal monstrosities that haunt you until you feel overwhelmed. Fear has the power to paralyze you, to steal away your potential and blessings, and it draws the greatness that God dreams for you right out of you. Fear steals your joy and keeps you focused on the probability of pain or danger, taking your attention away from God's promises. The by-product of fear is more fear and a bucketful of regrets and what-ifs.

Despite this there is another, healthy kind of fear, which is natural and instinctive. This kind helps us be aware and react to survive when we face *real* danger. For example, if you were running, and you saw a cliff, a healthy fear would stop you and keep you from falling off the cliff. Even the Bible speaks of the imminent fear we would feel if a lion were to roar before us (Amos 3:8). There's nothing wrong with having fear, but everything is wrong with living according to it.

The unnatural fear comes from the enemy, and its sole purpose is to hinder God's purpose for our lives and separate us from God.

Studies have shown that too much of this type of fear is detrimental to our health. The European Molecular Biology Organization (EMBO) reports

> There's nothing wrong with having fear, but everything is wrong with living according to it..

that "when we face a threat, our endocrine system releases [a combination of] hormones, which together with other signals turn up the systems we need to protect ourselves, and turn down those that are not immediately useful for survival. Although these systemic changes help protect us in the short term, they are detrimental if the stress persists."[4] The same report states that the effects of fear-related stress are associated with "a weakened immune system, increased cardiovascular damage, gastrointestinal problems such as ulcers and irritable bowel syndrome, decreased fertility, impaired formation of long-term memories and damage to certain parts of the brain, such as the hippocampus…fatigue, an increased likelihood of osteoporosis and type 2 diabetes, and aggravated clinical depression, accelerated ageing and even premature death."[5] The enemy knows this and uses it to fulfill his primary mission: to steal, kill, and destroy (John 10:10).

What's ironic about fear—and the reason I believe the devil likes to keep us in that state—is people who are in bondage to fear believe the lie that fear can keep them from pain, but in the long run fear causes more pain and suffering than what it prevents. Max Lucado says it beautifully in his book *Great Day Every Day*: "The presence of fear does not mean you have no faith. Fear visits everyone. But make your fear a visitor and not a resident. Hasn't fear taken enough? Enough smiles? Chuckles? Restful nights, exuberant days? Meet your fears with faith."[6] We must choose to live a life where fear does not control our every move, and we must allow God to direct our paths. After all, He always cares well for us (1 Pet. 5:7).

The good news is the enemy's destructive, paralyzing fear can only go as far as we allow it. The spirit of fear cannot control us without our permission. If it has managed to govern our thoughts, actions, and lives, we certainly have the power—with the Holy Spirit's help—to stop it and cast it out.

I grew up thinking fear was the opposite of faith and even heard sermons about it. Some even hinted that fear was a sin, which seems to be the subject of theological debate. However, even Jesus Himself experienced fear. Luke 22 and Matthew 26 tell the account of Jesus's agonizing fear right before being handed over to be crucified. His feelings were so intense as He faced imminent death that "His sweat became like great drops of blood" (Luke 22:44), a condition that is believed to occur "when a person is facing death or other highly stressful events."[7]

It certainly must have been terrifying for Jesus to know the gruesome suffering that lay ahead. Yet He has the right response to fear. He did not give in to it but held on to God's will, knowing it was best. This is the response we should all have when tempted to live in, by, and through fear: let go, and surrender to God's will. After all, "God has not given us a spirit of fear, but of power and of love and of a sound mind" (2 Tim. 1:7).

THE OPPOSITE OF FAITH

Rather than fear, the opposite of faith is doubt. As I mentioned, doubt is "a feeling of uncertainty, distrust." It is a hesitation to believe. On the other hand:

> Faith is the *confidence* that what we hope for will actually happen; it gives us *assurance* about things we cannot see.
> —HEBREWS 11:1, NLT, EMPHASIS ADDED

Also I love *The Message* version of verses 1–2 (emphasis added):

> The fundamental fact of existence is that this trust in God, this faith, is the *firm foundation* under everything that makes life worth living. It's our *handle* on what we can't see. The act of faith is what distinguished our ancestors, set them above the crowd.

Our faith has the power to keep us confident, assured, firmly founded, and with a good grip on God's promises for our lives. Doesn't it seem that the definition of *doubt* is the opposite of that of *faith*? While faith is confident, doubt is distrusting; while faith is certain, doubt is uncertain; while faith is firmly founded, doubt questions everything; and while faith is assured, doubt hesitates to believe. In Scripture we see that Jesus Himself described doubt as the opposite of faith. "O you of little faith, why did you doubt?" (Matt. 14:31; see also Matthew 21:21; Mark 11:23).

DOUBT, THE SUBTLE WEAPON

Doubt is a powerful weapon for the kingdom of darkness, and satan knows exactly how to wield it. Usually he'll wait for that moment when you've just been filled with a promise, whether you have received a word from God about what He has in store for you, have remembered one of His promises, or maybe even are approaching a time of fulfillment. Then and there, when God speaks to your heart, not much time will go by before you hear a tiny, faint voice in your head say something such as, "Did God really speak? Was this really God?" That is the voice of the spirit of doubt. In that moment we either let our faith arise and cast down doubt, or we lean in, continue to listen to doubt, and believe it.

During my walk with God I have encountered several reasons the enemy uses doubt.

Doubt extinguishes our faith.

The enemy knows that a person with strong faith isn't easily moved. Come trials, tribulations, and adversities, our faith is our firm foundation. Therefore the better founded we are in our unwavering trust in God, the closer we will come to Him in challenging times. The enemy hates that, so he tries to fill our minds with doubt in an attempt to eradicate our faith.

Doubt calls God a liar.

Think about this: When you doubt God, you question the veracity of His words. When you question whether something is true, you're opening yourself up to the possibility that it is a lie. However, the Bible is clear: God cannot lie (Num. 23:19; Titus 1:2). Although the enemy knows this, he has been doing everything in his power to get us to believe otherwise. Remember, satan has always wanted to be equal to God. It was precisely because of his pride in coveting the Almighty's sovereign place and his later rebellious attempt at overthrowing God that he was cast from heaven (Isa. 14:12–14). Since then, because he was not able to eradicate God from His throne, he's been impetuously trying to pull God down to his level.

The Bible tells us satan is "the father of lies" (John 8:44). Therefore when he throws doubt at us, what he does is call God a liar; he attempts to force God to come down to his level.

Because we are God's children and His most precious treasure— He gave everything to enable us to be with Him forever (John 3:16)—the enemy seeks to use *us* to pull God down to his level. He knows how much more it would hurt God if we were to doubt Him.

In essence by sowing doubt, what the devil seeks is to make us confess those doubts as if telling the Father: "I don't believe You. What You say isn't true. You're a liar." By giving in to doubting God and His word, we partner with satan in attacking God. Furthermore we uplift satan to God's place in our hearts, believing that his lies are truer than God's absolute truth. In the end when we doubt God, we help satan fulfill his desire to be the one enthroned over God in our hearts.

Doubt grieves the Holy Spirit.

The Holy Spirit is our Comforter, Ally, and Friend. He operates in truth and guides us to it. When we speak or act on doubtful thoughts toward God, we are allowing our lives to be led by the lie that God isn't truthful. This lie becomes our guide, which excludes the Holy Spirit. By doubting God, we push the Spirit away, rejecting Him as our truthful guide. If this happens long enough, we run the risk of grieving the Holy Spirit. Thus, progress toward our God-given purpose is set back, and we cannot move forward in God's perfect plan.

The Bible, in Ephesians 4:25, 30 (THE MESSAGE), says this about how telling lies and grieving the Spirit are connected:

> What this adds up to, then, is this: no more lies, no more pretense. Tell your neighbor the truth. In Christ's body we're all connected to each other, after all. When you lie to others, you end up lying to yourself....Don't grieve God. Don't break his heart. His Holy Spirit, moving

and breathing in you, is the most intimate part of your life, making you fit for himself. Don't take such a gift for granted.

Therefore we must be careful not to allow doubt to lead us into a life based on lies, but to let the Spirit of God guide us to all truth by eradicating doubt and welcoming God's truth into our every circumstance.

In life we will certainly face fear, and doubt will surely come along with it. One will paralyze our faith, and the other will bleed it out. Joyce Meyer said, "Negative minds full of fear and doubt produce negative lives, which can ultimately destroy your life."[8] Yet we have the power to identify fear and doubt, cast them out in Jesus's name, and choose to walk in the truth that trusting God is always the best way.

Pray Through Fear and Doubt

Fear and doubt should never be paralyzing agents in your life. If you're battling either or both of these, I invite you to say this prayer:

> *Dear Holy Spirit,*
>
> *I draw near to praise You with thanksgiving for being my Guide to truth. I am sorry for allowing fear and doubt to take hold of my thoughts and sometimes my words and actions. I renounce the lie that You aren't true and faithful to Your Word and promises. I choose to believe the truth and reject the lies. In the name of Jesus Christ, I cast the spirit of fear and the spirit of doubt out of my life, and I close any doors that I may have opened with thoughts and words of uncertainty and hesitation to believe You. I release myself into complete faith and trust that what You've said You shall also do in my life always.*
>
> *In Jesus's name I pray and believe, amen.*

Scriptures to Hold On To

Truly, I say to you, whoever says to this mountain, "Be taken up and thrown into the sea," and does not doubt in his heart, but believes that what he says will come to pass, it will be done for him.

—Mark 11:23, esv

Now faith is the substance of things hoped for, the evidence of things not seen. For by it the elders obtained a good testimony. By faith we understand that the worlds were framed by the word of God, so that the things which are seen were not made of things which are visible.

—Hebrews 11:1–3

But without faith it is impossible to please Him, for he who comes to God must believe that He is, and that He is a rewarder of those who diligently seek Him.

—HEBREWS 11:6

So do not fear; you are more valuable than many sparrows.

—MATTHEW 10:31, NASB

Part III

∽ WOMAN FOUND ∽

Chapter 5

∾ REBELLION ∾

There are two kinds of people: those who say to God, "Thy will be done," and those to whom God says, "All right, then, have it your way." [1]

A creature revolting against a creator is revolting against the source of his own powers—including even his power to revolt. It is like the scent of a flower trying to destroy the flower. [2]

—C. S. LEWIS (1898–1963)
CHRISTIAN AUTHOR, LITERATI,
AND FORMER ATHEIST

I WAS IN MY freshman year in college, and I'd become acquainted with the fast-paced teaching of my professors, which was very different from the seemingly coddling teaching style of high school. My major? Music, of course. I desired nothing more than to be a professional singer. So I enrolled for music education, specializing in classical vocal performance. Soon I stepped into the good graces of my professors and peers. "Your voice is…different," they'd say. On my first vocal evaluation my teacher told me excitedly: "You're a mezzo, but with the depth of a contralto and the highs of a lyrical soprano! What a phenom! I'm excited to see what we can do with this voice of yours." She then handed me challenging musical pieces that to me were a breeze to learn and perform. To my delight, my musical talent was opening doors for me. I was finally feeling as if I could be accepted.

Another delight was Romeo was always nearby. I spent every minute of my free time with him. So there I was, enjoying my two loves—music and Romeo.

My heart was full of dreams and aspirations, both professional and sentimental. Opportunities continued to present themselves with my studies and musical career, and I was determined to take advantage of each one. With great ease I became a soloist for the choir and concert ensembles at the university. The euphoria I felt every time I had the chance to perform made me feel as if I were on top of the world. In time I began receiving offers to further my career by recording professionally as a solo artist. Since I was a little girl, I'd dreamed of this kind of opportunity. Yet as much as I felt the urge to say yes to all my offers, I still struggled with fear. I feared that Romeo would feel left out, though I had been doing everything in my power to make him feel his best when he was with me. I did not want to risk him feeling uncomfortable or, ultimately, unhappy with me. I just couldn't bear the thought of him wanting to leave me over a disagreement. However, my dream to become a professional singer was also weighing heavily on my heart.

To help the two ends meet, I resolved to run every musical decision by Romeo. He'd decide for me, as I'd gotten him used to doing in every other area of my life. After all, it was easier to have someone else to blame if anything went wrong. He would choose for me, and I would follow. That was the dynamic. Things had carried on that way until the day he said no. I'd asked him about a golden opportunity to record my first full-length solo album. There were a million yeses resounding inside my heart; I really wanted to take hold of this chance. However, this implied that I had to meet with producers to start talking business, sooner rather than later. And as far as the producers were concerned, Romeo was not part of the equation.

"I have a meeting with the producers who are interested in recording my first album," I told him.

"When? I can go with you next week," he replied.

"Well, they want to meet tomorrow. And they want to meet with just me."

"No. If I'm not there with you, then you're not doing it. I need to be there. If I can't be there, then you're not meeting them."

"But I feel this is right. I can meet with them and tell you everything. But the only chance to meet is tomorrow."

"I already said no," he said with a stern, authoritative tone.

My heart sank. I stood at a crossroads. For nearly three years I had gotten used to him overpowering my thoughts and will. I allowed him to become my center, my guide, my ruler—what I should have allowed God to be. I was beginning to see the results of idolizing him, and they weren't pretty, especially not now that I was on the verge of seeing my biggest dream come true. I thought, "Thousands of people would die for a big break like this one, and I can't do it because he can't always be by my side at every waking moment?" It tore me right down the middle. One part of me needed Romeo in order to feel loved; the other part needed the stage in order to feel valued.

This situation opened a door I had purposely kept shut for our entire relationship; it was *the argument door*. Up until this point we had not had a single argument. In every disagreement I'd made sure to take whatever stance I knew would keep him happy and smiling because, again, I didn't want to do or say anything to lose him.

In so doing, I unknowingly created a monster that threatened to crush my long-awaited dream. Music had been my first love; I had more history with music than I could have ever had with Romeo. So yes, we argued. And lo and behold, the floodgates opened wide. All my pent-up frustration spewed right out. Every word I had shoved back down each time I did not speak up for myself, every case I had not made for my points of view to be defended or understood, and every boundary I had not set came rushing forth like a tsunami. We argued that day and the next day, and we increased the rhythm of discrepancies as time went by.

I was done trying to do anything just to please Romeo. At these first attempts at exercising autonomous thinking and decision making, things became increasingly difficult. And one day that submissive, subjugated girl broke out, becoming a woman resolute in following her dream, come what may.

So I began to walk toward that recording, going to my meetings with producers and creatives, whether or not he liked it. After all, it was *my* life, right? At this, our relationship became unhinged. Arguments turned into flat-out verbal attacks with terrible, abusive remarks. Our love was caught in the cross fire of screams, verbal spears, and many tears. Our courtship began to bleed out, until finally the love we had broke. This new, free-thinking Christine was someone he really didn't know—I had never let him see her until now. So after nearly three years together, in a bad argument over the phone he ended it once and for all.

At the abrupt clank of his hang-up, my heart was crushed— yes, the very heart I'd kept glued together with false hope in a guy who I thought could fill the voids left by my past, losses, grief, rejection, and fears. In that split second, phone still in hand, I could almost see, as if in slow motion, my heart falling to the ground then shattering beyond recognition.

And there it was again as if on cue—the agonizing sensations stinging and swelling, burning my insides. Pain was back. I put the phone down and tried to take a few steps, but my legs seemed to lose their ability to walk, and I collapsed. Fortunately my mother, who'd been listening in the other room and knew what terrible pain I must've been feeling, was there just in time to catch me before I hit the ground. For a few seconds I couldn't breathe. I tried to scream, but no sound came out, just pain.

The pain I felt was so intense it was silencing and deafening. It had returned, just as I feared. I'd briefly forgotten how much loss hurt, but this moment shoved me facedown into a cruel reminder.

Suddenly, when my breath almost expired, I let out a gasp and a gut-wrenching cry. Mom and my sweet sister surrounded me. I cried, and they cried with me. My sobs went on for hours, into the night, until my body couldn't take it anymore and passed out under the agony of a broken heart.

After a few months had gone by, I was finally recovering from my heartbreak. Romeo gradually became a thing of the past. I moved to a new area and set sail, finally devoting myself to fulfilling my dreams, which had evolved. I now wanted to be more than just a singer; I wanted to be a star. Still my moments alone in my tiny college apartment forced me to hear the sound of my faint, comatose heartbeat. It was in those moments I remembered and felt my pain more intensely. As I was immersed in heartache and disappointment, a voice in my head spoke to me. I wondered, "Is it my conscience? Is it me?" I know now it wasn't. This voice was different from my thoughts. It was distinct from the conversations I often had with myself.

Once, when I'd come home and crumpled on my bed, still grieving everything I'd ever lost, this voice spoke to me: "Oh, Christine. Look at you. Why are you crying? You shouldn't be! You should just accept the fact of who you are. Do the math. Your father preferred alcohol more than he did you, so he died. He abandoned you. Your mother remarried and moved you away from everything and everyone you held dear in New York, another abandonment. Your peers rejected you when you were little because you're different, so ugly, I'd say; they abandoned you. And now, after you gave your heart to Romeo, he broke it too. He also abandoned you! This must only mean one thing: you came to this world to be abandoned. No one wants you. You're...unloved."

I was desperate to escape this pain, which was amplified by a severe sense of loneliness. So listening to this voice seemed a better way to pass time than sinking further into desolate silence. To me these words seemed logical and convincing. After all, these things *did* happen to me, right? As I felt my emotions buzzing in self-pity, this adversarial voice carried on, making its case with a now firmer tone: "And where was God in all this? Where was He when your father died? Where was He when you were ripped away from home? When everyone rejected you? Or when Romeo was breaking your heart? Furthermore, where is God now?" Then came the statement that sowed a time bomb into my psyche: "If only God had prevented your father's death, none of this would have happened!"

These words sent a shiver down my spine. This voice made sense to my confused and depressed heart, and I began to slip into agreement with the voice, thinking, "How could God let my daddy die?" I couldn't see any other possible reasoning. I couldn't realize that my father's passing was a consequence of his actions and bad decisions. All I needed was someone to blame, someone I could expel my wrath on to. So I chose God; He'd be the target to which I'd shoot my pain. And I resented God. However, mine was an internal and quiet resentment—I'd been taught to never speak ill about God, so I didn't do so openly. I just listened to what this voice said.

I was unaware that this instigating voice was that of the very enemy of my soul and the prime hater of God. He had been taking advantage of my bleeding heart to infect it against God. Oblivious, I started believing those twisted words—with every fiber of my being. As days went by, the enemy's voice kept giving me ideas on how to get back at God for "what He had done to me." Soon my errant belief turned to action. But it wasn't an all-out, forward kind of action. It was passive, yet ever so aggressive.

At that point of my life I had become the worship leader at my church, a relatively large and influential congregation in my hometown. I was experiencing what it was to lead others in songs of worship. Each weekend many of those present at our church gatherings would sing praises with raised hands, humbled before God's presence. During times of musical worship some people got saved and some were even delivered. But to me moving people's hearts was just part of my duties. I came to think that if they felt anything at all, it was because I was the one taking them there. A bonus was the fact that I could dispose of the stage—I mean altar—to shine before many. To me it was just another platform where I got to do my thing—sing before many people, garnering wows, oohs, and aahs after each performance.

On weekends my life was all about church. I sang the songs, looked the look, and talked the talk. But on weekdays while away at college I most certainly did not walk the walk. I had resolved, based on my belief that God hurt me, that I would hurt Him back by doing everything possible to not please Him. So I began living a double life—purposely sinning on weekdays while away at college and maintaining the appearance of sacrosanctity each weekend at church. One side was alienated from the other. I was a faithful, religious church girl, yet I was lost, even in the house of God.

This double life led me into deeper levels of sin. Living mad at God drove me to compromise my faith and integrity. I erred in my thinking; I believed that God could not love me, so I resolved, in turn, to not love Him or anything that had to do with Him. This included my churchgoing family and friends. Whenever I'd hear the Word of God, I'd turn the other way, uninterested and sometimes opposed.

Despite my absorption into this sinful lifestyle my career began to flourish. Outside of leading worship at church, I occupied center stage in many influential singing positions in the university's music department. Also I was being called upon as a background singer for many well-known artists—some Christian—who performed in Puerto Rico. Doors opened for performances right and left. I took hold of each shot with poise and utmost charm. Where once I had been consecrated to serve and sing to only God, I did not care whether these performances

> I was a faithful, religious church girl, yet I was lost, even in the house of God.

were Christian in intent or not, frequently uttering the excuse, "Well, a girl's gotta eat, and I sing for what feeds me." Little did I know that not only was I feeding my mouth and ego with the pride that swelled in me from every gig, but also I was feeding my soul with bitterness, ever so present in my diva-like attitudes.

I'd come to live with an inner contradiction: my pride increased as my self-worth slumped. When it came to my career, I seemed to be on my way to a great start, but I was also sinking into a black hole of misery and depression. My only lifeblood was the apparent worth that others attributed to me based on my looks or talent. I was convinced that I was no one, that if I wasn't singing and being applauded, I was nothing.

That's when it happened. I'd lost sense of self. I stopped caring about me. I ceased to value myself; everything became irrelevant. Such was this lack of self-esteem that even suicide became a recurring contemplation. On several occasions it was more than just a thought. My pain-driven reasoning centered on finding means to escape the agony within me, but nothing was really working. I thought it was part of my identity to hurt, lash out, and make irrational decisions based on pain, only to hurt someone else. To say that I thought of myself as unwanted, damaged goods is an understatement. Therefore I came to consider that perhaps I would do myself a favor by ending my suffering. That way I wouldn't put anyone else through having to deal with my pain.

At moments, mostly when I was alone, I felt my walls closing in. My soul was suffocating as hope was being extinguished. At the same time, my choices and behaviors were to satisfy myself without restraint. I began to explore the world and its pleasures. Frequenting nightclubs and hanging out with people I'd just met became something recurrent and normal for me. Those dark and loud places are where I would go to self-medicate with alcohol to relieve my pain. The very thing that killed my father I started to see as a lifesaver. It made me forget. It numbed my pain. It hurt less when I drank, at least until the next morning, when I'd awaken feeling worse than before. I was becoming my father, but I wasn't sure that was a good thing.

To some, the sight of me was worth as much as a golden-egg goose. It was those people I gravitated toward most—people who said all the right things to stroke my pride. Among them I met a prominent producer, responsible for the takeoff of many superstars' careers. His words were music to my ears as he promised the world and all the fame I could ever want. To my great surprise he claimed he believed in my talent so much that he requested no money from me. Finally I saw my dream could come true, and in exchange for nothing, or so I thought. In no time I was fully invested in pursuing fame and recognition; that had become my primary target.

So when the time came when I was morally seduced to further a professional relationship, I complied. My integrity, purity, and honor were squandered for empty promises of massive stages and worldly glory. I valued myself at a fixed rate of 0 percent. Therefore giving myself away meant nothing to me; I believed I meant nothing anyway. I couldn't see myself as anything more than rejected, abandoned, unwanted, and unlovable unless I was on a stage singing to delight those I hoped would love me, if only for the melodies that came from my mouth, fueled by a bleeding soul. So that's what I did. I gave myself away, body and soul, to my sinful nature, holding nothing back. Rebellion had become my heartbeat, and sin, my sustenance, wrapped up in the sharp and aged ribbons of pain.

> The very thing that killed my father I started to see as a lifesaver.

REBELLION DOESN'T HAPPEN OVERNIGHT

It is important to know that rebellion doesn't just happen overnight. You don't wake up one morning after being a good, genuine, pious person and simply turn into the opposite. Rebellion is a subtle spirit. It comes and whispers hateful thoughts into your mind, and if you listen to them, you start acting them out. Such was the case with *my* life. The roots of rebellion usually go far deeper than we think, oftentimes passing through several generations before reaching us. They take time to sink in. But when they do, we find ourselves committing the same acts toward which we felt so much rebellion. For example, I became rebellious because of my father's death, the cause of which was alcoholism. Yet my rebellion moved me to do the very thing that gave way to my pain in the first place. Blinded by rebellion, I allowed the lifestyle that destroyed my father's life—and that caused me so much bitterness—to take the reins of *my* life.

ROOTS OF BITTERNESS

Rebellion is birthed from resentment and bitterness. When resentment lodges into our hearts, it produces bitterness. Then, when bitterness takes over our thoughts—and thus our actions—it moves us to rebel, usually against the object of our resentment. I believe wholeheartedly that we would have no reason to rebel if there were no bitterness in our hearts. That's because our thoughts affect our actions. The more you think about doing something, the closer you are to doing it, and finally, if you do not change that thought pattern, you succumb. When bitterness is a harnessed, nagging thought, rebellion is the resulting action. Bitterness is the cause; rebellion, the effect.

Bitterness has the power to entangle our lives in such a way that we lose sight of our moral compass. Scripture says:

> ...looking diligently lest any man fail of the grace of God; lest any *root of bitterness* springing up trouble you, and thereby *many be defiled*; lest there be any *fornicator, or profane person*, as Esau, who for one morsel of meat sold his birthright.
>
> —HEBREWS 12:15–16, KJV, EMPHASIS ADDED

Bitterness leads to the defiling, or corrupting, of a person, including lustful behavior such as fornication or profanity. Entering into these sinful behaviors causes a greater mess because lust fulfilled causes a heightened sense of anger, bitterness, and hate. Such was the case with Amnon, son of King David, who Scripture tells us raped his sister Tamar. After he gave in to his lust, he became enraged toward her (2 Sam. 13).

When there is rebellion, one must find the root of bitterness feeding it and cut it out. Otherwise it will renew itself. Upon investigating the roots of my bitterness, I discovered many interesting generational issues in my lineage. As the story goes, my grandfather, my father's father, was a singer with musical aspirations. He and my grandmother married very young and had my first uncle, quickly followed by my father, who came as a surprise to a young couple that could barely make ends meet. To support his family, which was now bigger than he'd expected at that time, he gave up singing altogether and worked in construction. Perhaps this is what caused resentment in my grandfather, which he especially directed at my father. Several years passed before they had more children, and during that time my grandfather's frustration grew, which he often unloaded on to my father in the form of verbal or physical abuse. Both my grandmother and father became bitter toward my grandfather. A few years later, after having two more children, my grandfather died, consumed by a terminal illness, and had had little time to establish a proper relationship with my father. This grief, combined with a deeply anchored bitterness, likely led my father to become rebellious, adopting addictive behaviors. He even had a few problems with the law in his teenage years. After a wake-up call with the law he tried to turn his life around. He joined the US Air Force. During his time of service sadly he witnessed the atrocities and traumas of the Vietnam War. His bitterness, now increased, plunged deeper into his heart. All he had learned and experienced created a hardened root that would seep deep enough to reach down to me and mine unless cut out. My bitterness came long before my father passed and long before he even knew what bitterness was. Who knows what root of bitterness that had gone unnoticed had been growing from my ancestors.

Maybe there are roots of bitterness in your life too. And perhaps they are sprouting a rebellion in your life as well. If so, you must find their origin and renounce it to take the proper step toward God's peace. Only then will you be free from rebellion.

LOST IN THE HOME OF SALVATION?

It is always a sensitive subject when someone speaks of a Christian who has failed, or "fallen from grace." Even after the many years I've testified about it, the subject still has a tendency to make people cringe a little. Not many people seem willing to talk openly about it. Perhaps it's because more people than care to admit it are trapped in a double life that includes hidden sin. Maybe they do not want to risk their sin being revealed. Or possibly they've already found deliverance but are so ashamed of their past that they don't want it known publicly. All these reasons are understandable.

However, the sad truth is many more people than we are aware of within the church need salvation just as much as those who do not go to church. I find it interesting how Jesus would often preach more to the religious people of His time than to those who did not profess to know God. He once said:

> Not everyone who says to Me, "Lord, Lord," shall enter the kingdom of heaven, but he who does the will of My Father in heaven. Many will say to Me in that day, "Lord, Lord, have we not *prophesied in Your name, cast out demons in Your name,* and *done many wonders in Your name?*" And then I will declare to them, "*I never knew you*; depart from Me, you who practice lawlessness!"
> —MATTHEW 7:21–23, EMPHASIS ADDED

A bitter, rebellious heart can still work for God and even be used by God in tremendous ways—as I was—but not be saved in the end. Bitterness drives you to defile yourself and others and lose track of morality. This, in turn, makes you even angrier, leading you into an endless cycle of anger and rebellion. But you can overcome rebellion with God's help. Works will not get us saved and into heaven (Eph. 2:8–9); that happens only by allowing Jesus to be our sole Savior and Ruler, relying completely on Him to steer us clear of sin by His grace. This can only be done by maintaining a true relationship with God, based on loving Him with all our hearts, souls, strengths, and minds and loving our neighbors as ourselves (Luke 10:27).

PRAY OVER REBELLION AND BITTERNESS

Maybe you are facing some form of rebellion. Perhaps bitterness is clawing in your heart. Maybe you've been through so much that you're mad at God. Whatever you are going through, do not let bitterness and rebellion get the better of you. If you're battling a bitter heart or rebellious tendencies, I invite you to say this prayer:

Dear God,

I'm mad, I'm sad, and I feel like lashing out, even with You. But I've lived with pain and disappointment long enough. Forgive me for blaming You for my pain. I know now that there's more to it than just pointing fingers. Forgive me for my attitude of anger and resentment. Also forgive me for my defiance toward correction from You and other authorities. I can see clearer now, and I know my defiance is rooted in bitterness. I renounce that root and the belief that made me harbor it. In Your name I cut all generational ties to it. I will carry bitterness but will replace it with Your love and peace. I repent of my rebellious ways, and I ask for forgiveness for the ways I may have defiled others or myself by harboring bitterness and rebellion. I am free in You, and I anchor my soul on to Your Spirit. As for those who have wronged me, I know that You are my Justice and Truth. You take care of me in the presence of my enemies, and in You I am saved and kept safe. Lord, thank You for hearing me and healing me. I release my life and my heart into Your hands. Fill me with the Holy Spirit so I may resist the temptation to rebel again.

In Jesus's name I pray and believe, amen.

SCRIPTURES TO HOLD ON TO

He is the Rock; his deeds are perfect. Everything he does is just and fair. He is a faithful God who does no wrong; how just and upright he is!

—DEUTERONOMY 32:4, NLT

The commandments of the LORD are right, bringing joy to the heart. The commands of the LORD are clear, giving insight for living.

—PSALM 19:8, NLT

God sets the solitary in families; He brings out those who are bound into prosperity; but the rebellious dwell in a dry land.

—PSALM 68:6

I will walk in freedom, for I have devoted myself to your commandments.

—PSALM 119:45, NLT

Chapter 6

∞ GRACE ∞

A man does not get grace till he comes down to the ground,
till he sees he needs grace. When a man stoops to the dust
and acknowledges that he needs mercy, then it is that the
Lord will give him grace.[1]

—D. L. MOODY (1837–1899)
AMERICAN EVANGELIST, SPEAKER,
AND MISSIONARY

CLASS LET OUT much later than I'd expected, and I was running late. I rushed my way through traffic in an attempt to arrive at rehearsal as close as possible to the start time. This would not be just any rehearsal. This one would change everything.

A friend had called me in to be a lead background vocalist for a special concert at the Centro de Bellas Artes (Performing Arts Centre) in San Juan, the most prestigious stage in Puerto Rico at the time. It was for a Christian event, one of the first allowed to be held at such a grand arena. Only the big names played there. And now I'd be there, even if just behind a background vocalist's stand. Just the thought of being seen performing on this glorious stage made my fantasies of grandeur swell. I could almost taste my illusions of fame and success. So of course I'd accepted the invitation. After all, I *am* a Christian, right? It was only appropriate that I'd give an immediate yes, "to serve the Lord well." At least that's what I kept telling myself to justify my prideful thoughts.

When I arrived, rehearsal had already started. I walked into the building in haste and with my head held high. Almost at the rehearsal room door I was briefly deterred by the beeping of my phone. It was a text message from one of my acquaintances, from the opposite side of decency. We'd been planning to meet that night after rehearsal to do things I'd gotten used to doing in hiding. Bad things. Shameful things. I quickly replied, "Got it. Tell you when and where in a sec," and picked up my pace heading into the rehearsal room.

A POWERFUL PRESENCE

Suddenly, upon walking through the rehearsal room door, a deep shock hit me inside and startled me for a moment. Entering the room I found that rehearsal was fully engaged. But the sound... it was familiar, but then so unfamiliar. I took a good look at everyone. Eyes were closed, voices were raised, and those who had a free hand lifted it up high. I seemed to have crossed a threshold into another dimension of sorts. It felt as if I had cut right through the atmosphere, causing an internal sonic boom that shook my entire being. A presence—one that I recognized but did not know—was there among those musicians and singers. *He* was there and made it known to me.

It was as if an invisible light cut through the darkness and grabbed hold of me. I felt terrified at the thought that this light could somehow uncover my darkness. I began to shake inside. I wanted out—and quick. I thought if I stayed, everyone would be able to see me for what I really was as soon as the song ended and they opened their eyes. I could not bear the thought of anyone finding out that evil had gripped me.

Just as I was about to scoot back toward the door and slip out unnoticed, the song ended. All eyes opened, and it was too late to leave. The lead singer, whom we'll call David, saw me and smiled. He quickly came to greet me. I responded, "Hi! What's going on in here is so beautiful! But I was just on my way out." Trying to invent any excuse to run from there, I carried on, saying,

"Eh…it's that I have a last-minute situation I need to go deal with. It's kind of life or death, and I have to go now. In fact, I'm so sad to tell you that this situation won't allow me to be a part of your event after all. I'll send in a substitute for the next rehearsal, who will cover me, but I have to go. I can't do it anymore. Just pray for me."

At that he looked at me and smiled for a second. Then he said: "Christine, don't worry about your situation. When you walked in, the Holy Spirit spoke to me. He told me what you're going through." I must have opened my eyes wide in shock. Then I became so afraid that my fear of having my sin exposed was about to manifest. I thought if the Holy Spirit had told him what I had done in the past few days, or even what I was getting ready to do that night, I'd be shamed in front of everybody and kicked out to the dirt, where I belonged. But to my surprise David said: "But that doesn't matter. What matters is that you don't go. Just stay here and worship with us. When we finish our rehearsal, we'll pray together, and God will do something amazing. You'll see. Just please stay with us. Don't go."

I thought about it for a moment and agreed to stay. Within a few minutes my battle truly began raging. As I remained there, I kept getting text messages from the other side, asking for details about our midnight rendezvous. I felt a strange panic grow inside me at the mere sight of these messages. I became so scared about going out and doing sinful things. Hands trembling in terror, I was unable to even answer the messages. Evidently the perfect and powerful presence being manifested in that room was already starting to affect me. For the first time in a long time I experienced conviction of my sins. For the first time in a long time I could see how wrong I was, how divided my heart was, how conflicting my life had become. So I sat there and went through rehearsal, all the while trembling inside as the worship of God's children increased and took over in that little room.

DIVINE INTERVENTION

When we were done, we all decided to head out to eat at a nearby diner. I got in my car, still stunned from what I had just experienced; put my key in the ignition; and, before turning it, placed my hands on the steering wheel. In a moment I had become fed up with the turns my life had taken. Yet pride wouldn't allow me to admit it. So my way of asking for help came out as a snotty rant, an ultimatum of sorts. I shot out words like daggers: "Listen, God, if You're real, and if it's true that You see me, love me, have a plan for me, and all that stuff the Bible says, You have until midnight tonight to show me—that is, if You're even listening, if You even exist at all. If You don't, I'm done! I'm leaving church and diving into the world for real this time. If You don't care enough to show Yourself to me before the day is over, then I don't care enough to hold on to this church-girl facade. And if I end up lost in the process, then so be it!" After I finished my outburst, I could hear that little mischievous voice in my mind say: "You really told God, didn't ya! He sure got a piece of your mind. Now watch. He won't do a thing because He's not even listening." With a huff and a puff I started my car and headed out.

Upon arrival at the restaurant we could see it was full of church folks, some we knew and some we could just tell were churchgoers. Certain telltale signs distinguish some churchgoers from other people. In some people the Holy Spirit can be seen in them as their faces light up. Other churchgoers are distinguishable by the way they dress or speak. I could tell the place was full of believers.

Shortly after we sat down, I saw a lady walk in alone and be seated in the corner across from us. As she walked from one side of the restaurant to the other, it gave me a chance to take a good look at her. I was raised quite conservatively and was taught Christians should adhere to a dress code. I was taught a Christian lady wore skirts and not pants, little or no jewelry, and no makeup or vibrant nail colors. Her hair was to remain long and uncolored, and the style should be simplistic. I'm sure it was all well intended. Most likely this belief system came about as an effort to keep others from stumbling. It also honors those who come to the Lord needing restoration, perhaps battling lust. Yet it is true that to many—though not all—people, through the years this dress code became more than a supportive expression of compassion for others. It became a lifestyle indicator, something necessary to be considered someone who "knew" God, without which many weren't even considered saved. Sometimes the physical appearance mattered more than having an intimate relationship with God. So I made sure to *look* Christian among Christians, though at the time there was really no sight of Christ in my heart.

At the sight of that woman I cringed. She was wearing a multicolor blouse-and-pant set with bright stilettos. She had bleach-blond hair and wore red lipstick, vibrant purple and blue eye shadow, peachy-red blush, and a beauty mark accented to the left of her nose. Her hands bore many chiming bangles and bracelets, and her fingers sported long red nails and a few sparkly rings. The sequins on her blouse beckoned even more of my attention as she walked across the room.

Needless to say, the least of my thoughts was that she was a Christian. I thought of every religiously judgmental thought I could possibly formulate. I even thought having such flamboyance made her pagan. Even seeing the birthmark that she ever so intensely accented on her face made me think of her as a witch. The pharisaical nature I had well developed in practicing my hidden sin came at her with every ounce of mental strength I had. In my head I was ready to burn her at the stake of my self-righteousness.

The damaged soul inside of me had flared up with criticism, cynicism, sarcasm, hate, pride, and judgment. Upon losing sight of the woman, I looked at my watch to see that it was nearly a quarter past eleven. I had told God that He had until midnight to do something that showed me He cared. Yes, I had given Him a quite daring ultimatum in the nastiest attitude possible, and yes, I doubted He'd even care to reply, but my heart was in dire need of Him. Deep inside I yearned for even the slightest sign that He was there, that He could bypass all my failures and come to my rescue. So I was alert with anticipation. I thought I hated God, but I also needed Him and hoped that He indeed had heard and was on the way.

With expectancy I signaled David from across the table to remind him of his promise to pray for me. Right away we went outside and stood under a tree in the parking lot. My sister, who had met up with us for dinner and who was probably the only one I'd made privy to the kind of life I was living, joined us. Standing under the tree, David began to speak to me from the Word of God. For a few moments it was almost as if he were preaching a sermon prepared just for me. And for the first time in a very long time it began to make sense to me. I hung on his every word. It felt as if my soul were as hungry as a newborn past her mealtime and was finally being fed the Bread of Life. I slowly began to feel a strange awakening inside me.

After a few minutes he said, "I'm going to pray for you now. Close your eyes and raise your hands. I'm going to place my hand on your head, and God is going to do something wonderful as we pray." I raised my hands and bowed my head, eyes closed, as he laid his hand on my head and said, "Father, in the name of Jesus…" That instant I heard the door of the restaurant swing wide, abruptly hitting the end of its swing. Immediately following was the clack-clack, clack-clack sound of high heels. The sounds were enough to steer away my attention, as I could hear the steps coming closer and closer. All of a sudden, I felt them stop cold right before me, and a woman in front of me said, "This says the Lord to you!"

I cracked one eye open to catch a glimpse that made my heart sink. It was the woman I thought was not Christian! As it turned out, she was a prophetess of God. She began to speak to me as God's very mouthpiece: "I am the Lord your God. I *do* exist. I *am* real. I *do* love you. I *do* have plans for you. And if you allow Me to, today I will show you."As she spoke those words, led by the Lord, I felt a thousand currents run up and down my spine, spreading to the end of every extremity, physical and spiritual, and I began to shake uncontrollably. I could feel the weight of God's glory falling on me like the heaviest blanket that could exist. It embraced me and crushed me at the same time. In that moment I became aware of His sovereignty over everything. I was not in control, and I had finally realized I never was.

The woman continued speaking God's message regarding my life with words so certain and true. I had never been witness to such a strong prophetic anointing as this. How much detail she used in speaking about the condition of my life—places I'd frequented, people I'd hung around with, feelings I'd had, decisions I'd made, and even thoughts I'd had, many of which I had never uttered to anyone—was so overwhelming it almost felt as if this woman had been following me around for the previous months of my life.

> "I am the Lord your God. I do exist. I am real. I do love you. I do have plans for you. And if you allow Me to, today I will show you."

Yet I knew deep down inside that it was He and not she who had been in pursuit of me all this time; I just hadn't realized it before. It was God who knew me and watched me stumble through it all. He'd been patiently waiting for me to give Him the chance to show me and teach me to stop looking at my own broken desires and start looking at Him. Taking advantage of my openness, God answered me. It was life-giving and oh so moving to find out that God *did* care about me enough to respond to my specific, even snarky, prayer and to do so in such a unique and unexpected way. His intervention was nothing short of the expression of His goodness, delicate gentleness, and unconditional love wrapped up in a single moment. He made me know for the first time in a long time that there was indeed still hope for a wretch like me.

Though I was faced with the difficult truth of how lost I really was and how much I'd sunk into filthy sin, I could feel God's grace washing over me, and I couldn't help but embrace it. I felt His mercy. I did not feel shamed, rejected, pointed out, or condemned. I felt...*loved.* Upon receiving this revelation, I could not contain myself, so I wept. I wept like a child who had fallen to the ground, bruised. That child within me raised her hands to a big, strong Daddy in total surrender. And I felt as if His great big arms began to lift me from the dirt, envelop me, and hold me in a lingering embrace as if to say: "Oh, my beloved child, I'm so sorry. You've hurt yourself so badly. But come; let me clean up these wounds, heal you, and make you ready to run free again." After what felt like an hour God was still speaking to me through that woman. I was still shaking, overwhelmed, and overcome by such great love, mercy, and grace. At this point my body was bent forward under the invisible weight of every word, and I was nearly on my knees. I could not contain what I was feeling, the steady stream of Christ's blood washing my filth from the inside out. Toward the end of this encounter with the Lord, He said something that forced me to make a choice—the biggest, most important one of my life.

Two Paths

In His great humor, since I had given God that ultimatum, He responded with one of His own: "Today there are two paths placed before you. You must choose one now and live the rest of your life with your decision. The first path is Mine, the way of My heart and My will for your life. In it every one of My promises will come true in you. If you follow My way, I will heal your heart, restore you, and lift you up as an example of what My love can do, of how I can take something broken and make it new and beautiful.

"If you follow My path and will for your life, I will take you to the nations. You will lead them to Me by the thousands, and they will find Me and be saved, healed, and restored because they'll see Me in you and know that I am real. When you sing, I will heal hearts of stone and open up the heavens as you lead them into My presence. I will heal every single one of your wounds, and there will not be a trace of your past left to pain you. As I lift you up and you continue to do My will, I will provide for your every need; you will never want for food, clothing, or any of the resources needed to fulfill My will. My wealth will be yours, for I will be your Father, and you will be My child.

"Our relationship will grow closer than you could ever have imagined. I will guide your every step, and I will not allow for you to be confused or deceived. We'll become so close that you will stand and speak, and I will do—and I will speak, and you will do. At times there will be no need for words because you will get to know My will so well; our desires will merge into one. Our hearts will sync to the same heartbeat, and we will walk at the same rhythm. This is *My* way, a perfect path that I designed just for you. It is My desire for you to choose this way, and if you do, My presence will be with you always until the end."

These words reverberated in my heart as the sweetest sound I had ever heard. I longed for precisely that—for God to come in, take over, fix my life, and handle me with perfect care.

Just as I was gathering the courage to lean God's way, He carried on: "And then there's the second path, which is the way of *your* heart and *your* will for yourself. You have a great heart, very sensitive, but your heart deceives you. You've followed what your deceitful heart has dictated all this time, and it's brought you to the path you are currently on.

"If you continue down this path, some things will definitely go your way. I've gifted you with talent and the power to fulfill your dreams. Therefore in this path you will reach your goals and scale the great heights of your career. You will come to possess that fame you've so desired, and much fortune will come with it. A point will come when hundreds of thousands of people will follow you. They will sing your songs, come to your shows, strive to imitate you, and idolize you as they would a goddess of your generation. Everything you've ever desired in this world will come to you.

"I will make sure you're kept safe, not because of your decision to choose this path but for the sole reason that I have made a promise to your mother that I would do so. But know this: If you choose the path of your own will," He said firmly, "My presence will *not* go with you."

The sound of those words, "My presence will not go with you," pierced deeply into my heart, clawing into the very core of my being. Suddenly a sharp pain shot through me in every sense—spiritually, emotionally, and even physically. Feeling as if a million daggers were stabbing my heart, despair took hold of me. My chest felt as if it were going to split open and bleed out, and the most horrible notion hit me like a ton of burning bricks: "How could I possibly survive without Your presence? I just can't! I can't…and I…I won't!" I could hear the voice of my own spirit screaming within me: "Nooo! I can't live without Your presence! I'll do anything—whatever You say, whatever You ask. I…I surrender! I surrender my dreams and everything I ever wanted. Nothing matters anymore! Take it all, but I beg You, don't take Your presence from me! I choose to follow Your path, but please stay! I can't live without Your presence…and I don't want to live without Your presence! I give myself away to You. Please don't take Your presence from me! Please!"

I realized the hopelessness and despair those who have crossed into eternity without God's presence must feel. The mere thought of a life void of God's presence was the most terrorizing thought to ever cross my mind. I felt as if I were going to die if I held on to my way just a moment longer. The words inside me spilled out: "No, God! Don't take Your presence from me. I'll do anything You ask. I surrender! I lay down all my dreams, all my desires, all my wishes. I don't care about any of it anymore! You can take them all away, but please don't take Your presence. Please! I choose

Your path. I'll go Your way; just please stay! I can't live without Your presence. I *won't* live without Your presence."

That day a divine appointment was made. God showed up, just as I'd asked Him to. My life changed forever, but not because I'd gotten a step closer to fame, as I had thought would happen, but because I took a step closer to the Father. That day in August 2003 I encountered the perfect, redeeming, embracing, and forgiving love of God. That day I looked grace in the eye and fell in love with my Father. That day the prodigal child came home, and I was born again, a daughter of the living God, the great I Am. That day I was forgiven, and my sins were forgotten. That day I chose God's way—and I'm never turning back.

———————•———————

THE PRICE OF GRACE

Grace is an undeserved favor that God has poured out on us. It is free for all mankind. We can do nothing to earn it or repel it. It is simply a gift from God. Grace is something we cannot acquire or produce on our own. Yet God, knowing this, still gives grace, love, and mercy, allowing us to obtain salvation through Christ's sacrifice on the cross. You see, without grace we would have no way to reach God.

God may have decided that grace is free for us, but it certainly cost Him to give. The price of grace was paid with the greatest tender: the life and blood of the Son of God, Jesus Christ. God came down, became flesh, lived a mortal life, sacrificed Himself to die a most horrible death, and resurrected on the third day, all to make grace fulfill its purpose of enabling us to receive salvation and a place with God forever.

The Bible says, "For by grace you have been saved through faith. And this is not your own doing; it is the gift of God" (Eph. 2:8, ESV). Grace is a gift that leads to salvation, which is another gift for which we need faith. The Scriptures also say that *"without faith it is impossible to please Him*, for he who comes to God must believe that He is, and that He is a rewarder of those who diligently seek Him" (Heb. 11:6, emphasis added). In my experience with grace I had to reach out to God and believe He was there for Him to intervene. God knew what I had been through. He knew how much I needed Him. However, I was not able to have an encounter with Him until I made a true admittance of His existence and invited Him into my life. After I exercised faith, I found salvation but could only find it by grace. It was by His grace that I was able to cross paths with Him at the right and perfect moment. Had I not accepted or believed that He was there and I needed Him, I would probably be lost in my own world of self-destruction, or worse.

Perhaps you are like me. Maybe you've been searching for ways to win your way to salvation by acts, with or without God's presence. Maybe you keep finding yourself frustrated because your relationship with God simply isn't what you wish it was or is non-existent. If that's the case, I've learned that a better way to please God is to have faith in Him, trust that He's there, and truly surrender your life to Him. That's when grace works best—when we acknowledge we do not deserve God's love and mercy but still need it to live.

TRUE REPENTANCE

An encounter with God such as I had always needs a catalyst to work; it's called repentance. It's easy to confuse repentance and remorse. With both of these comes a deep, heartfelt conviction of being wrong, but there is an important difference between the two. *Remorse* comes from a place of guilt, while *repentance*, though it brings the acknowledgment that you've done something wrong, is a *decision* to change. So repentance results in transformation, while remorse does not.

In Mark 1:15 Christ says, "The time is fulfilled, and the kingdom of God is at hand. Repent and believe the gospel" (MEV).

The word *repent* here comes from the Greek *metanoeó*, which means "I repent, change my mind, change the inner man (particularly with reference to acceptance of the will of God), repent." [2] Repentance is what happens when you say, "I'm no longer going that way in my life; I'm turning around and going the other way." It's what happened to me when I decided not to continue pursuing my own will and dreams but to follow Christ, come what may.

When we've committed sin, we may feel remorse or guilt for the things we did wrong. However, we are not able to be free of that sin until we repent, or change our ways so we do not commit that sin again. The decision to turn our lives around is ours. That is something God cannot do for us. I believe that is why God showed me the two paths I could take in life. Having a clear perspective of where I was and where I would end up helped me realize I desperately needed to change my ways to be truly free. I'm so glad God's grace enabled me to see where I was standing and make the right choice for my salvation.

Today you may be standing at the crossroads of your own paths in life. I assure you, God is calling you to go deeper into the path that He has drawn out for you so carefully. He wants to be closer to you. He wants to see you fulfill His purpose for your life. He wants you to have life and live it abundantly. The only way to get there is by repenting the right way, always leaning toward God's will and not your own. After all, He created us and knows best what path we must take to truly embrace grace, be saved, and thrive in Him.

PRAYER OF GRACE

While embracing grace is amazing, it is not always easy. To embrace grace we must surrender and come to realize we are nothing without God. We must also realize there is nothing we could do to cause God to love us any more or less. He simply loves us and pours out His grace on us freely. The best we can do is love Him with everything and seek Him more every day. If you are finding your way to embrace God's grace and surrender fully to Him, I invite you to say this prayer:

> *Dear heavenly Father,*
>
> *I come before You acknowledging that I am nothing without You. I need You in order to live, breathe, and become who You want me to be. Today I surrender to You. I give You my all. Take my life, my dreams, my goals, and my past, and draw me a clear path to Your heart and will. I acknowledge that my works alone cannot gain me salvation, that it is not by my works that I am saved but by Your grace, the undeserved favor that You freely give. I repent of my old ways; I do not want my will for my life but for Your will to be done. Teach me how to listen to Your voice and follow Your lead with humility and abandon, that I may reach deeper into Your heart and know You.*
>
> *In the name of Jesus I pray, amen.*

SCRIPTURES TO HOLD ON TO

For by grace you have been saved through faith. And this is not your own doing; it is the gift of God.

—EPHESIANS 2:8, ESV

Let us then with confidence draw near to the throne of grace, that we may receive mercy and find grace to help in time of need.

—HEBREWS 4:16, ESV

And now I entrust you to God and the message of his grace that is able to build you up and give you an inheritance with all those he has set apart for himself.

—ACTS 20:32, NLT

We believe that we are all saved the same way, by the undeserved grace of the Lord Jesus.

—ACTS 15:11, NLT

Chapter 7

∾ RESISTING ∾ TEMPTATION

Ability to resist temptation is directly proportionate to your submission to God.[1]

—ED COLE (1922–2002)
MISSIONARY, EVANGELIST, AND FOUNDER
OF CHRISTIAN MEN'S NETWORK

PURE BLISS FILLED my heart. I was in love. Not like I'd ever been before—not like with Romeo, not like with music, not like with my dreams. This time I was in love with Love Himself. I had finally been found by the only One who could fulfill me, understand me, and keep me safe and on the right path throughout my life. I had hope again. I had joy. I'd been redeemed, and my sins were washed away forever. To say that I felt as light as a feather was a tremendous understatement.

After my encounter with God I knew I needed a change of scenery to leave behind my double life and start out on the right path of restoration and nearness to God. So I began taking steps toward that change. I'd already begun experiencing God's guidance, just as He had promised. I started truly seeking God—praying, reading His Word, and listening carefully to every Scripture, sermon, and worship song I could get my hands on. I was determined to stand my course deeper into God's heart. My sinful ways would no longer be the axis of my decisions.

Then, shortly after, the real test began. As if out of nowhere, I began receiving phone calls from every one of those people I'd previously "hung out with" to sin. I started letting the calls go to voice mail, but the messages became interestingly appealing. My mind seemed to be playing tricks on me. Thoughts of lust and immorality, pride and entitlement, anger and friction, inefficiency and inadequacy, fear and depression, deception and manipulation, disappointment, alcoholism, suicide, and even sinful appetites I had never before indulged in came roaring and pulsing through my brain.

My sinful ways would no longer be the axis of my decisions.

I thought: "What's going on? Why is this stuff coming to me now, just when I am determined to fix my life with God? Why am I tempted with all this now?" In that moment of great weakness and vulnerability it seemed easy to just give in. But I had decided to go the other way, down the new path I'd promised God I would follow. I ran to Him instead of my heart's crooked desires. I prayed: "Lord, help me. These temptations are getting too hard to handle. What should I do? Jesus, please just come." When I spoke His name, I could feel Him steadying my heart as I sensed Him speaking one simple word: "Resist."

Immediately that still, small voice breathed peace inside me. Still the concept of resisting was something I couldn't really comprehend in this scenario. It frustrated me, as did the deliberations that bounced around in my brain. "Resist? How would I be able to? How could I just resist? Wasn't there more to it? Wasn't I supposed to fight this with something stronger? Wasn't there some sort of spiritual weapon to defeat these feelings and desires?" I thought there was more to it, but still I chose to obey God. I chose to resist, come what may. The battle became fierce. The enemy came with waves of temptation through my thoughts and my randomly bumping into people from my past who would try to persuade me to go back to my old ways. Some nights I'd even have nightmares in which I was committing horrible sins or replaying scenes of my worst sins. Pestering judgments aimed at the center of my mind. A full-force battlefield was inside my head. I tried to kneel to pray, and something would distract me as if on cue. Still I wrestled through with the help of the Holy Spirit, with whom I was just beginning a beautiful acquaintance. I'd made up my mind; for the first time in my life I'd elected to resist temptation for the sake of following the God I love, no matter what. I was not going to give in! The more I felt tormented by thoughts of my past, the more I would cling to Jesus. The more I feared having to deal with my dirt, the more I trusted God. There was only one constant in this whirlwind of mental and spiritual warfare: God loved me enough to rescue me from my ways, and I would *not* go back.

One afternoon I received a call from a friend who had been praying for me since she learned of my breakup with Romeo. We hadn't interacted much for a long while. But my birthday was coming up, and she wanted to catch up. She shared with me that she'd been sensing for some time that I was not all right and she needed to pray for me. She'd been interceding for me for months. Amazed, I gave her the news of my miraculous encounter with God. We could hear each other's sniffles over the phone from tears of joy! I was saved, truly saved, this time. She invited me to come to her church that Friday, and I gladly accepted.

Friday came, and it could have been the heaviest my body had ever felt. It was difficult just to get out of bed. It was one of those days when things didn't go as expected. I faced temptations, bad thoughts, and even heavy arguments throughout the day. I almost called off the whole invitation to the new church. But I felt that I needed to go. I felt that if I could only resist a little more, I would be blessed if I went. So I swam against the current of my day and went. I stepped out of my car and walked toward the big tent that was the "sanctuary," where I heard people worshipping. I walked in looking like a deer in headlights, marveled at how strongly I felt God's presence. Then I looked for my friend.

An usher must have seen me looking confused and asked if

he could help. I said a friend had invited me, and since he happened to know her, he quickly directed me to my seat, where I planted myself and basked in the spiritual light emanating from that church. There was something different from what I was used to. It was louder, and the worshippers were much more passionate than those at any other church I had attended. Most importantly I felt God's presence so close that I could almost reach out and touch His face. In the midst of all this the pastor had the microphone in hand and was worshipping and singing. This was indeed new to me. It revolutionized my thinking. "A pastor not waiting for a 'proper' transition and jumping in to worship with the rest of the church?" I wondered.

As if he could read my mind, the pastor turned around and came right to me. He began to tell me what he felt the Lord spoke to him about me. God spoke to me again! He told me of the great things He had in store, that He was pleased with my decision to resist the devil, and that He hasn't left me but was just enabling me to become fully restored. God's glory was so dense around me. For a moment I felt as if no one else but the two of us were under that pretty tent. When I regained my composure after tears had been flooding my face, several people embraced me. I felt loved and not rejected. I felt as if it was OK to be me and stand where I was in my process because God was right there with me. In that instant I took a good look around, and I understood something new. I thought, "This doesn't feel like church; it feels like *family*."

CAUTION: GHOSTS AT THE DOOR!

The past has a way of haunting us, and even more so when we turn from old lifestyles and truly decide to improve the way we lead our lives. Moving forward is sometimes harder to do if we've made grave mistakes in the past. For me it was hard to deal with the shame and guilt I felt as a result of my sins. At times I felt as if my mind were under siege; I couldn't think about anything else but what I had done.

This mental battle usually came in two forms. The first was a strong sense of guilt because of my sins. This guilt drove me to resign to the belief that nothing I could do would ever bring me closer to God, that I had ruined every chance to have intimate communion with Him. It was a more subtle way to deplete my self-worth and entice me to revert back to old behaviors. The second, however, was more direct. Seductive thoughts reminded me of how good it felt to do what I wanted to do. Accompanying these thoughts were carnal inclinations and a whole lot of me, myself, and I.

I had made up my mind to obey God and resist these invading thoughts and desires. Though that was not easy, in doing so, I learned how to be guided by the Holy Spirit and emerge from this inner conflict victorious. The Lord directed me to His Word to understand what was really going on during that season of initial restoration. Scripture speaks about what happens to a person who is delivered from being under the influence of spirits that operate evil within them:

> When an unclean spirit goes out of a man, he goes through dry places, seeking rest, and finds none. Then he says, "I will return to my house from which I came." And when he comes, he finds it *empty, swept, and put in order.* Then he goes and takes with him *seven other spirits more wicked than himself,* and they enter and dwell there; and the last state of that man is worse than the first. So shall it also be with this wicked generation.
> —MATTHEW 12:43–45, EMPHASIS ADDED

This passage is so important to understand when we are pursuing a righteous life. When we do not have Christ as the King and Savior of our lives, we are under the reign of satan, ruler of the opposite kingdom, which holds us in bondage to sin. When we come to the Lord and give Him our lives, we are no longer slaves to our sins, our past, and the influence of these spirits of darkness. As we receive Jesus in our hearts and proclaim Him as our Savior, the Holy Spirit comes to dwell in us (Rom. 8:9), God's perfect love casts out all fear (1 John 4:18), and sin is erased by the blood of Jesus (Rev. 1:5). Thus, surrendering our lives to Christ makes our lives "empty" of sin, "swept" clean from our past, and "put in order" by the Holy Spirit, as Matthew 12 describes.

The evil, impure spirits that had a hold on our lives in the past are cast away when we invite Jesus into our hearts. However, they *do* come back around. Since they may not easily access our lives when coming alone, they bring stronger, more malevolent spirits to try and infiltrate our lives, binding us to sin again, making it seven times more difficult to eradicate the second time. That is why I believe the Lord was asking me to resist. Had I given in to my past and sins, I would have opened a door to these spiritual influences to take hold of my soul again, making it even harder to be freed once more.

Another lesson I learned was that resistance is the centerpiece of successful spiritual warfare. Some people tend to think of spiritual warfare in the same way they do physical warfare. Yet when it comes to the fight in the spirit, we do not use the same strategies and weapons as with physical warfare. There are simply no tangible weapons we can wield and be done with our spiritual enemies. In Ephesians 6 we see a perfect depiction of this:

> For *we do not wrestle against flesh and blood*, but against principalities, against powers, against the rulers of the darkness of this age, *against spiritual hosts of wickedness in the heavenly places.*
> —EPHESIANS 6:12, EMPHASIS ADDED

Second Corinthians 10:3–6 (emphasis added) is even more explicit as to the type of weapons that are not effective spiritually:

> For though we walk in the flesh, we do not war according
> to the flesh. *For the weapons of our warfare are not carnal*
> but mighty in God for *pulling down strongholds, casting
> down arguments and every high thing that exalts itself*
> against the knowledge of God, *bringing every thought
> into captivity to the obedience of Christ,* and being ready to
> punish all disobedience when your obedience is fulfilled.

In these two Scripture passages we can see whom we fight
against and that our weapons are not physical. But the question remains: What weapon *is* effective? Moreover, what is the
best weapon against the enemy? This is where it gets really good!
When the Lord taught me this, it blew me away. James chapter 4
holds the key:

> Therefore *submit* yourselves to God. *Resist the devil, and
> he will flee* from you.
> —JAMES 4:7, MEV, EMPHASIS ADDED

I know of no place in the Bible where it speaks of anything
besides submitting to God and resisting the devil being powerful
enough to cause the devil to flee from us. You see, it is when we
submit to God that He enables us to resist temptation. It is by
His power working in us that we can stand against the devil's
ruses. We cannot stand against the enemy on our own. We are
only human and are weak. But it is in our weakness that He is
strong and in our admittance of our weakness that He becomes
stronger in us (2 Cor. 12:9–10).

HOW TO RESIST SUCCESSFULLY

It's great to know the *who, what, why,* and *where* of our situations
to overcome them. But if you're like me, the *how* is extremely
important to put your plans of freedom into motion. How can we
successfully resist temptation and walk away from sin?

It is true that more often than not our human inclinations tend to lean more toward sinful behaviors than righteous and pure ones. In Romans 7 the apostle Paul is speaking to the Romans about the law (God's rules) in contrast with our fleshly desires. He says:

> I don't really understand myself, for I want to do what is right, but I don't do it. Instead, I do what I hate. But if I know that what I am doing is wrong, this shows that I agree that the law is good. So I am not the one doing wrong; it is sin living in me that does it. And I know that nothing good lives in me, that is, in my sinful nature (flesh). *I want to do what is right, but I can't. I want to do what is good, but I don't. I don't want to do what is wrong, but I do it anyway.* But if I do what I don't want to do, I am not really the one doing wrong; it is sin living in me that does it. I have discovered this principle of life—that when I want to do what is right, I inevitably do what is wrong. I love God's law with all my heart. But there is another power within me that is at war with my *mind*. This power makes me a slave to the sin that is still within me. Oh, what a miserable person I am! Who will free me from this life that is dominated by sin and death? Thank God! *The answer is in Jesus Christ our Lord.* So you see how it is: In my mind I really want to obey God's law, but because of my sinful nature I am a slave to sin.
>
> —ROMANS 7:15–25, NLT, EMPHASIS ADDED

We live in a world corrupted by sin; sin is in our nature. To help us steer clear of our natural tendencies to sin, God's law—the Ten Commandments (Exodus 20)—gives us guidelines to follow. Until the day arrives when we go home to heaven and no longer must live in a battle, we are subject to stumbling over our iniquities and failings. I commonly hear people say it is "so hard" to follow God and not sin. As a public figure I constantly get asked, "How do you stay close to God and live purely for Him?"

My answer is something I discovered as I was learning to run to God and depend on Him: "Love God and love people."

The Word says in Mark 12:29–31 (emphasis added):

> Jesus answered him, "The first of all the commandments is: 'Hear, O Israel, the Lord our God, the Lord is one. And you shall *love the* Lord *your God with all your heart, with all your soul, with all your mind, and with all your strength.*' This is the first commandment. And the second, like it, is this: 'You shall *love your neighbor as yourself.*' There is no other commandment greater than these."

Think about it: when you love someone—truly, deeply, whole-heartedly love someone—you strive to please that person. I've seen people change their lives around to accommodate what the beloved prefers. It is the same with God. Love—for God and for others—is the ultimate power we need in order to stay away from sin. When we truly love God, we will do anything and everything necessary to make sure He's delighted in our lives, just as when we truly love others, we'll do anything to not sin against them. Therefore the key to successfully resisting temptation and sin is to love God and people so much that our love makes us second-guess sinning against them.

Maybe you're reading this and thinking, "How could I love the Lord so much like that?" The answer is simple: nurture your relationship with God every day. Talk to God, read His Word, and walk with Him throughout your day as you would with the love of your life.

PRAYER TO RESIST TEMPTATION

We all face temptations in life. Even Jesus did during His time
on earth. He knows better than anyone what it means to face
weaknesses and overcome them. Holding fast to God is the best
way to overcome and not fall into temptation. Whenever you are
tempted, I encourage you to pray a prayer like this:

Dear Jesus,
   *Thank You for opening my eyes to the truth of Your love
for me. I acknowledge that I am just a human in need of
You to overcome my weaknesses and frailties. I turn to You
because You know what it's like to be a person living in this
sin-ridden world. So today I choose to keep my mind on
You and Your plan for me, not my own. I choose to pursue
Your heart and not my earthly desires. I surrender again to
Your will, and I ask You, Holy Spirit, to guide me into all
truth. I surrender my thoughts, my desires, my actions, and
my future to Your will. And I confess that I love You, Lord,
more than anything. Help me fall deeper in love with You,
love others as I love myself, and stay far away from sin and
close to You.*
   Jesus, in Your name I pray, amen.

SCRIPTURES TO HOLD ON TO

No temptation has overtaken you except such as is
common to man; but God is faithful, who will not allow
you to be tempted beyond what you are able, but with
the temptation will also make the way of escape, that
you may be able to bear it.
                                    —1 CORINTHIANS 10:13

Resist him, steadfast in the faith, knowing that the same
sufferings are experienced by your brotherhood in the
world. But may the God of all grace, who called us to

His eternal glory by Christ Jesus, after you have suffered a while, perfect, establish, strengthen, and settle you.

—1 PETER 5:9–10

Therefore submit yourselves to God. Resist the devil, and he will flee from you.

—JAMES 4:7, MEV

Keep awake (give strict attention, be cautious and active) and watch and pray, that you may not come into temptation. The spirit indeed is willing, but the flesh is weak.

—MATTHEW 26:41, AMPC

Chapter 8

◇ RESTORATION ◇
AND INNER HEALING

When God forgives, He at once restores.[1]

—THEODORE EPP (1907–1985)
AMERICAN CHRISTIAN CLERGYMAN,
WRITER, AND RADIO EVANGELIST

We are co-creators of our destiny alongside God. God leads, but we have to choose to let God lead.[2]

—DR. CAROLINE LEAF
COGNITIVE NEUROSCIENTIST,
AUTHOR, AND SPEAKER

I FOUND A CHURCH I could call home. I knew in my spirit I could grow stronger in my faith and relationship with God there. It wasn't a place where I was needed for leadership, nor were any expectations placed on me. I didn't need to worry over anything other than loving God. As it turns out, I knew the usher who received me at the church entrance. He was my best friend's boss five years earlier. Seeing a familiar face among all those underneath the tent was refreshing.

A good friend of mine invited me to join her, her boyfriend, and some others from the youth group at a nearby restaurant. I was hesitant to go since I didn't like the idea of being a third wheel. My interest changed, however, when my new acquaintance—the usher who was also the pastor's brother—said he'd come too. At least now I'd have someone to talk to other than a very in-love couple in between smooches. After Romeo, being witness to any kind of public displays of affection made me uncomfortable and brought up painful memories, so I steered clear of them as much as I could.

After chatting for a while in the church parking lot, we headed out. When we arrived at the eatery, we realized there was no room for us to sit at the big table with the rest of the group. So the four of us resigned ourselves to a small booth in a corner of the room. My girlfriend sat beside me, and we immediately continued to catch up. Talking about redemption, hope, joy, and the Lord came easily to me. And the way God spoke to me at church that night had me awestruck. We discussed just about everything we could think of. Our eyes filled with tears as we talked about hardship. We hugged many times and expressed joy at the hope renewed by God's grace.

Then, as is common when girls are catching up with their girlfriends, the question came. It caught me off guard, as we had been talking about spiritual matters. She ever so politely and with great interest asked, "So Christine, how's it going in the love department?" There was a pause. I felt a huge knot squeeze my insides. Within a split second my mouth spouted hate: "Wait a minute!" I looked deep into her eyes as if to find her very soul and yank it out. "I know what's going on here, and I'm not having it!" I said, turning around and shifting my eyes among the other three at my table. "Let me tell you something. Men are jerks, dirty jerks. They're only seeking one thing from a woman, something that I'm not willing to give!" Then I turned around to the only guy without a girlfriend at the table and, with my index finger raised at his eye-level, spewed, "And nothing personal, *Carlos*, but you're a man, so that goes for you too! So just in case you had any ideas, I'm not interested!" Then I quickly turned toward my girlfriend and, with sass, added, "Now please, let's change the subject." An awkward silence swept over our table until dinner was served.

Two days later she called. It was my birthday, and I was supposed to meet her for a last-minute get-together and a little
"happy birthday to me" time. I couldn't make it due to a sweet
surprise celebration with family and friends. In the midst of my
telling her all about my cheerful night, her phone died. My friend
borrowed a phone from the first person she could and called me
back. I answered the call from the unfamiliar number to hear her
on the line. She said, "Oh, by the way, Carlos sends his birthday
wishes. He was the one who let me use his phone to call you back!"

Oh boy; I felt a plot unfolding. I thought, "What is she doing?
Now my number is in this guy's phone!" But of course I was not
going to ruin a perfect day with an argument. So I directed my
inner aggression elsewhere, toward my new favorite scapegoat,
Carlos. "Carlos said to send me *what*? How was that guy raised?
Didn't his momma teach him manners? You can tell him that
birthday wishes aren't sent; they're given! Sheesh!" Always the
peacemaker, she repeated my statement to Carlos in a much more
polite and less scolding way. Soon he was on the phone, apologizing for something he wasn't even guilty of, and at the same
time he was unknowingly apologizing for my soul's pain, which
he had nothing to do with.

My sass soon simmered down at the tone of his voice as he said:
"I'm sorry. I just didn't want to interrupt your chat. I know you've
been catching up with her after a long time. But happy birthday!
How was your day?" In that moment I couldn't help but admit
that this guy was still friendly, even after my lashing out the other
night. A little hesitant, I slowly began to share how my day went.
Soon the joy of the celebration took over, and I was smiling. Then
the chat turned into a real conversation that continued on and on.

Four hours later we finally hung up when his phone beeped
indicating the battery was about to die. After our good-byes
I just looked at my phone, thinking. I'd never had a good, neu-
tral, and enjoyable conversation with a guy I'd just met without
there being a secondary interest or agenda. This was certainly

new and unusual. I couldn't help but think, "Who is this guy?" I felt a spark of hope. I began to see that maybe not all was lost for my heart, that I could probably have a good friend in this guy. Before going to sleep that night, I prayed, "Father, You know that I don't really want to relate to anyone besides You. I'm afraid that if I open my heart, I'll be hurt by a man again and run the risk of straying from You once more. Please help my heart to not be deceived. I don't want a boyfriend right now, but if it is Your will, let it be, but only with the man who will be my husband. And please speak to me, tell me clearly so there is no room for doubt."

The following week we were going to meet some of the youths from my new church. We'd planned to go enjoy the beautiful bio-luminescent bay called La Parguera in Lajas, Puerto Rico. Upon meeting at our rendezvous, I was surprised to find that everyone had canceled except the four of us who dined together a few nights before: my friend and her boyfriend, Carlos, and me. I felt a chill rush down my spine at just the thought that maybe this was a plot to force me to spend time alone with Carlos. Though it turned out not to be anything of the sort, the circumstances nearly pushed me to think the opposite because we ended up going together in his car. The lovey-dovey couple sat in the back seat, and I was left to sit in the front beside Carlos, who would have to brave the storm of my ice-cold treatment the entire drive. Every one of his kind gestures was responded to with cutting words or rolling eyes. One thing surprised me, though: despite my snarky and defensive attitude his didn't change. His kindness didn't waver.

Remembering our long conversation the other night and com-bining it with recent events caused my thoughts to clash into each other. I could see a handsome guy with a great attitude, upbringing, and relationship with God. But also I could see the open wounds in my heart that needed to heal.

After we arrived and boarded the boat that would take us into the bay, Carlos and I moved to the closest rail to look at the water. We soon lost sight of my friend and her boyfriend. And there I was in an awkward predicament. "What am I going to do with all this time on this empty boat with this guy...and alone?" I thought. Right away I resolved to go watch the bay from the top rails. And he, as any gentleman would do, didn't let me go alone. Realizing his intention to stay with me, I thought, "I'd better pass the time in conversation. Maybe that way time will go by faster." And that is what we did. We began talking as we leaned on the railing in awe of the bioluminescence in the water. Only a few minutes had passed before we were entrenched in a conversation that seemed to take on its own course. We talked about faith, the Bible, and the future, and I at no time felt asphyxiated by the notion that this guy was pursuing a romantic relationship with me. I found that I could be myself with him without having to try to impress him.

The ferry came to a stop in the middle of the bay. In the stillness of the night I could hear the soft babbling of the sea. At that point we were discussing God's callings for each of our lives. I lifted my eyes to look at Carlos. The full moon shone behind him, and his silhouette fell in perfect accord with the silvery reflection on the wavy water. Then something surprising happened. I heard the voice of the Holy Spirit, audible and clear. He spoke to me in a tone I'd never heard Him use before. I could sense a tad of sarcasm in His voice, as if to point out something obvious, and I could hear Him smiling through His words as He said, "Well, behold the father of your children!"

Immediately my eyes opened wider than ever, both physically and emotionally. God has answered another prayer! A veil of fear had been ripped away from my eyes, and I could finally *see* Carlos, the beautiful man right in front of me, speaking oh so securely of how God would take him to minister to and serve the hearts of so many. When we got back to the dock, I looked up and saw light. It wasn't just the artificial light from the bulbs on the boardwalk, which allowed me to see his face more clearly, but there was light in my heart. It was as if I could see him for the very first time—his chestnut hair, his grayish-green eyes, which dazzled me with each blink. His beautiful smile and contagious laughter made my world stop every time he laughed. His tall stature and strong figure made me feel safe and protected as we walked beside each other. I had to contain myself so he wouldn't notice the spontaneous sighs escaping me when I looked at him.

In that moment I put my guard down. I'd decided that where before I'd fallen in love having the foolish heart of a teenager, now I'd allow myself to begin falling in love having the heart of a woman, guided and protected by the Holy Spirit. I'd never before felt a love so real, pure, and true for a man as what I was beginning to feel for Carlos that day. The feeling was even stronger now that I knew God was in the equation.

As time passed, my faith grew stronger, and my relationship with the Holy Spirit was more intimate than ever. I began taking grand steps toward becoming whole again. Slowly I saw God's love reassemble me, my beliefs, and the core of my identity. My friendship with Carlos deepened. He became my best friend, support, prayer partner, and confidant. He knew everything about me and did not judge me, as so many had before.

As time went by, we grew even closer, and he expressed that he had developed feelings for me, as had I for him. I still had not told him what I'd heard the Lord speak to me about him that evening on the ferry. I'd save that secret for later. We began dating, something that was a miracle in my eyes. How could a great guy like him love a broken girl like me, especially after knowing all the things I had done? To this day I still cannot wrap my head around that thought. One thing is for sure: I could see Jesus in Carlos; he loved me for me, not anything else. And I fell head over heels in love with him.

After dating for some time, we felt the Lord impress on our hearts that we were "the one" for each other. Carlos asked me to marry him, and without hesitation I said yes. No other man in my life respected me, loved me, and protected me the way Carlos did. God is so good that, in His grace and despite my failures, He saved a man for me who was beautiful inside and out, who had a pure heart, loved God deeply, and was full of wisdom, compassion, drive, passion, and all the strength I didn't have.

God had cleaned my dirty hands to be able to hold a great treasure: the heart of this man. And I was going to do just that, remain pure to honor God and Carlos. Having been redeemed, I saved myself for Carlos, and we practiced abstinence until marriage. It was not easy, but our love for God was so much greater than our physical desire for each other. God helped us keep our minds on His plan and His Word. Therefore we were able to start our marriage with the right foot forward.

Our wedding day came. On that beautiful summer day the Holy Spirit breathed life and favor on us. We also felt His covering throughout our honeymoon and back home. We experienced what it is to have Jesus at the center of our lives. We went into the Word of God together and prayed together. One day we saw the truth and beauty of Scripture in Ecclesiastes:

> It's better to have a partner than go it alone.
> Share the work, share the wealth.
> And if one falls down, the other helps,
> But if there's no one to help, tough!
> Two in a bed warm each other.
> Alone, you shiver all night.
> By yourself you're unprotected.
> With a friend you can face the worst.
> Can you round up a third?
> *A three-stranded rope isn't easily snapped.*
> —ECCLESIASTES 4:9–12, THE MESSAGE,
> EMPHASIS ADDED

That's what we became—two strands intertwined with our best friend, the Holy Spirit. It was He who united us, made us strong, and guided our new household. When we arrived home from our honeymoon, I finally told him what God had spoken to me on that full-moon night at La Parguera. With his big, beautiful smile he said: "I also knew it. I asked God for you, and He brought you to me. And it's forever." During those first few weeks of marriage we were filled with God's blessing in our newly established home.

Four years later my spirit had grown stronger as my soul remained anchored on the hope I'd received in God. My relationship with Him indeed was growing in intimacy, just as He said it would. After I had already learned the wonders of forgiveness and practicing it, the world lifted off of my shoulders. I soaked in this newfound freedom through forgiveness and made it a habitual part of my life.

Throughout those years I'd become free from the shackles of rancor, resentment, hate, and bitterness. I was able to run free and live life abundantly. My relationship with God became a priority. In my spiritual growth the more I came to know of God, the more of Him I needed. My soul's hunger couldn't be satisfied by anything less than God's presence. Furthermore, God released me from my pride and healed my expectations of myself. I thought I'd ruined my chance of ever singing for Him publicly again. Yet God taught me it was His plan all along for me to do just that, but with a renewed perspective of glorifying Him rather than myself. He taught me the ways of humility and asked me to continue singing professionally, but only for Him this time. God orchestrated every aspect of my ministry and singing career, as He did my spiritual life. He allowed for me to release my first solo recording, then a second. During that season Carlos and I could not have been more humbled to see how God can take a broken person and make her whole again, blessing thousands of other people in the process.

During that time we focused on trusting God, and, as Ecclesiastes 9:10 says, anything we had the opportunity to do with God we did with all our might. He blessed us so

> My soul's hunger couldn't be satisfied by anything less than God's presence.

much. Our obedience to Him became greater and broader, to the point where Carlos and I felt directed by the Lord to move out of Puerto Rico. Just like Abraham, we left behind all we knew and held dear for the sake of the cross and directing other people to it. We moved to Orlando, Florida, and followed God's lead in everything. The more we surrendered and believed Him, the more the Lord blessed us with provision and success in the work He commanded us to do.

In the newness of living by faith, I began to understand that there is indeed so much more that God has for us than what we could ever ask Him for. Above all, there was more of Him to be revealed to me, and I pursued His presence wholeheartedly. In my pursuit I was determined to deepen my relationship with the Holy Spirit. I ran with all my might toward fulfilling the insatiable thirst I had for His presence. During this time I entered into a season of much more prayer, communion with God, and fasting. It wasn't because I wanted anything *from* God; it was because what I desired *was* God. With every fast I completed, I had wonderful experiences with the Lord, and the level of the revelation of Him in my life increased dramatically. In that season He truly became my closest Friend, and He remains that to this day.

On one occasion, when I set out on a twenty-one-day partial fast, I became ill. I thought I had a stomach bug, but it became progressively worse day by day. Over-the-counter remedies didn't alleviate the bad symptoms, which included the involuntary elimination of food, shivers, and even blood coming from my body. I couldn't hold anything down but water. I talked to doctors, who thought I had bacteria in my intestines, and I took the medication they prescribed. Yet the pain and other symptoms did not let up, and the examinations did not show anything definitive.

Since I was a recording artist and worship leader, I'd have to toughen up and fulfill commitments to minister at places I'd been scheduled at for some time. I went to each event I had scheduled within those twenty-one days, and God used me to touch people's hearts with my testimony. I even saw people healed by His power as we prayed. But for nearly three weeks, I was still ill, unable to eat, sleep, keep anything down, or use the restroom without terrible pain.

I cried out to God for healing. I recited every Bible verse I could think of about healing. I prayed earnestly for the pain to go away and for me to be well again, but nothing changed. I became desperate. Then I became annoyed. Then I nagged God: "What is this? Where are You, God? How is it possible that I pray for others, and You heal them, but I'm still sick? Why am I in this bed without energy or health, even when I make an effort to follow and obey You? It's not fair. Why don't You just heal me?" I received no answer.

Something inside pushed me to carry on. I knew I couldn't break the fast or stop seeking God. I knew deep down that after a great battle comes a great victory. At least I held on to that hope and continued my fast, come what may.

On the final night of my fast I was still terribly ill. I had lost a substantial amount of weight and was very weak. Still I was at a church event waiting for the microphone to be turned over to me to sing that night. As I waited, I received a text message from my sister saying: "Mom's terribly sick. Something's wrong with her pancreas. We don't know what, but the doctors say it looks bad. She's being taken to intensive care. Please pray." I felt my world crumble. Thoughts shot back and forth in my head. I was sick and at the end of myself, but I understood that I must have been going through a process. But Mom? So sick the doctors are worried? What was going on? The thought of something happening to my mom was too much for me to bear.

I could feel despair sinking its claws into me. For a moment I wanted to leave, run from that place and my commitment, but I didn't think I had the energy to do so. I felt helpless, hopeless, and alone, tempted to crawl under a pew in a fetal position and stay there until I died. I was falling and barely grasping the end of my rope.

Suddenly I felt something twinkle inside of me. The Holy Spirit brought a memory verse to mind that is repeated in Psalm 42:5 and 43:5: "Why, my soul, are you downcast? Why so disturbed within me? Put your hope in God, for I will yet praise him, my Savior and my God" (NIV). With the rise of that Word within me hope surged up like a spring of water. I realized there was nothing I could do. I couldn't heal myself or my mother. I couldn't even afford to go see my mother in Puerto Rico.

So I gave up, gave in, and surrendered. I chose to make God—not my adverse circumstances—the center in that moment. I decided that worship was the only thing I *could* do, so I did it. I repeated to myself, "For yet I will praise Him, my Savior and my God." Even if He wouldn't do a thing, I would still praise Him for who He was.

I sent this reply to my sister's text: "Don't worry. We're praying. God is in control." Then I buried that phone as deep as I could into my handbag. Then and there I raised my hands in surrender, and I worshipped as if that were my last moment on this earth. I praised God with as much passion and abandon as I could and with every bit of brokenness I had.

Suddenly I heard God speak, clear as day. As I worshipped, He said, "Now *that's* what I was waiting for!" I let out a spurt of laughter, and I felt joy—the kind Nehemiah 8:10 says is my strength. In that instant my faith aligned perfectly with my thoughts, my belief, and God's will; I knew everything would be all right.

The next morning I was at church leading worship like never before. I was still sick, but my praise sure didn't let that show. After the service one of the musicians, a sweet, humble man, prayed a simple prayer of healing over me—and I was healed! The pain went away, my body felt normal again, and I could eat solids for the first time in three weeks. Needless to say, that Sunday was a full day of praises in my house!

However, the true challenge came the next afternoon. I jumped in the shower mid-morning and took advantage of the alone time to talk to God. I thanked Him and reassured Him that I trusted Him and His will. In that conversation I recalled something. The memories coming to the forefront of my mind were haunting. They had been buried in my subconscious for a long time. These were memories that...I had been sexually molested at age five.

I must have suppressed these memories to cope with the events that followed pertaining to my father's illness, his death, our new family members, and relocation. In the game of pick-and-choose, my brain had buried that terrible trauma under the rug of my subconscious, but now God had brought it to the surface.

The memories came all at once. They hit me like a ton of bricks. I relived every memory as it came forth: the room, the sounds, the smells, everything. It was all so vivid. I felt a knot in my stomach, a weakening of the knees, and a loss of breath. A deep-founded fear was finally showing its root.

I got to marry the love of my life, who's always been gentle and caring. However, ever since our honeymoon, I felt a strange fear of being close to him. I would often cringe or be startled if he would wrap his arms around me. I tended to feel way too bashful and awkward when opportunities arose to be romantic or close as man and wife. And I always feared any kind of intimacy. I wanted us to truly be one, as the Bible says, but there was a distance, a disconnect that I couldn't explain. I thought it was—and would always be—the remnants of my past sins; I'd accepted that it was an old soul injury I would just have to live with. But now everything had become clear.

I'd fallen to my knees under the running water in the shower, feeling the impotence of that five-year-old girl. I remembered every occasion and the faces of my molesters and tried to wash off every bit of filth that was thrown on me, a helpless child. I felt used, like damaged goods, and I could now see why I still felt so unlovable.

When I was done remembering and processing these hor-rible memories, the Holy Spirit came over me like a blanket. In between painful sobs I felt how my tears would meld with a hope and a peace that truly did surpass my understanding. I could hear the Lord's sweet voice saying: "Forgive them. I helped you, remember, so you can be free. Now forgive them." So there on the floor, naked and with nothing left, I forgave, and I was set free.

That day I felt God's embrace holding me together, restoring yet another broken piece of me. That night, for the first time, I truly felt my husband's embrace, and I was no longer afraid. Less than two weeks later my mother was released from the hospital because her body had been astonishingly restored back to health. Restoration is such a beautiful thing, yet it is only possible when we let go and let God.

FORGIVENESS: A MARVELOUS KEY TO RESTORATION

Many of us have heard the phrase "Forgiveness is the key." But it seems more easily said than done. In fact, forgiving can be very dif-ficult to do. Personally I've had major issues with holding grudges. My emotions have always run deep, for better or for worse. I feel deeply and love deeply, but I also hurt deeply. Therefore I've had the inclination to hold my pain closely, which isn't without its challenges.

For instance, before I learned the freedom that comes with for-giveness, I used to cringe at merely hearing the word. If someone told me to forgive someone, my gut response was, "Never!" Unforgiveness often becomes a comfort—it certainly was for me.

You may ask, "What's so special about forgiveness? Why does that person deserve my forgiveness? Do you know what he did to me?" All these are valid points. The pain behind them is very real. However, I learned a few things about forgiveness in my journey to restoration.

First, let's look at what Luke 6:37 says about forgiveness: "Judge not, and you shall not be judged. Condemn not, and you shall not be condemned. *Forgive, and you will be forgiven*" (emphasis added). When we draw near to God, we can only go as far as we are willing to sacrifice.

Have you ever seen the rope that holds bungee jumpers? It's a long elastic rope that holds them back. Though it may stretch far, it always pulls the jumpers back no matter how much force they put into their jump. Imagine now that unforgiveness is like that rope tied around you. If you try hard to draw near to God but haven't forgiven, that rope may stretch, but just as you're about to grab hold of new things in God, you'll be pulled back. Unforgiveness is like dead weight that cripples your soul, impeding it from moving forward and closer to God.

Let's take a more in-depth look at Luke 6, specifically verses 32–33 and 35–38 (emphasis added):

> But if you love those who love you, what credit is that to you? For even sinners love those who love them. And if you do good to those who do good to you, what credit is that to you? For even sinners do the same....But *love your enemies*, do good, and lend, hoping for nothing in return; and *your reward will be great*, and you will be sons of the Most High. *For He is kind to the unthankful and evil. Therefore be merciful, just as your Father also is merciful.*
>
> *Judge not*, and you shall not be judged. *Condemn not*, and you shall not be condemned. *Forgive*, and you will be forgiven. *Give*, and it will be given to you: good measure, pressed down, shaken together, and running over will be put into your bosom. *For with the same measure that you use, it will be measured back to you.*

At the beginning of my walk to freedom, this was probably my least favorite Bible passage. That was the case until I started believing God, obeying God, and putting it into practice. Here are a few things the Holy Spirit taught me about the truth enclosed in this scripture:

"JUDGE NOT"

Jesus clearly said we must not judge, and we would not be judged. To judge is to form a judgment—"an opinion, conclusion, or belief based on the circumstances before one's view."[3] To judge is "to form a judgment or opinion of; decide upon critically; to infer, think, or hold as an opinion."[4]

Before entering into full itinerant ministry, I worked for an attorney for a couple of years. In that law office I learned that for a judge to pass proper judgment, he or she must be presented with all the facts surrounding the case in question. Even when that happens there are times when the facts do not assure a correct judgment for even the most meticulous and upright of earthly judges.

When we feel ill will toward someone—even if that person has hurt us—we are casting judgment on him. Entertaining ideas such as, "I'm never going to be like that person," "I'll never do what they have done," or "At least I'm not as bad as they are; I've never done *that*," reveals a judgmental mind-set.

But is it possible that we can know every fact about a person's physical, emotional, mental, and spiritual life? Absolutely not! Only God knows all. Therefore only He is qualified to judge. When we judge, not only are we disobeying God's Word, but we fall terribly short in our judgment, causing more harm than good. Furthermore we accumulate more things for which we shall be judged. After all, we are far from perfect.

"CONDEMN NOT"

Condemning usually goes hand in hand with judging. While judging is the act of forming bad opinions and beliefs about someone, condemning is expressing those unfavorable opinions. Judging usually is thought inwardly, but condemning is expressed outwardly. When we condemn, we essentially point the finger at others, marginalizing them, declaring them unacceptable, sentencing them, and strongly disapproving of them.

Condemnation is a nasty form of rejection. I believe Jesus said not to condemn because He is a God of unity and not division. Also, He knew that whenever we push someone away, someone else, in turn, will reject us and push us away, causing a chain reaction of soul wounds and the adverse effects that come with these.

Scripture says in Romans 8:1, "There is therefore now no condemnation to those who are in Christ Jesus, who do not walk according to the flesh, but according to the Spirit." If we are truly of Christ Jesus, we have no dealing with condemnation. We should just let God, our perfect Judge, take care of our circumstances in His perfection and righteousness. If we do condemn, then as the Bible promises, we shall be condemned also. I don't know about you, but I sure want to steer clear of being condemned.

"FORGIVE"

The dictionary defines *forgive* as "to grant pardon for (an offense); absolve; to cancel or remit (a debt, obligation, etc.); to cease to feel resentment against."[5] In addition, the Lord taught me more about forgiving. When we forgive, we become free from that emotional weight pulling us away from God. Forgiveness isn't designed to favor the forgiven but to bring freedom and healing to the *forgiver*.

When we forgive, we choose to bring down our own judgments and condemnations against others, and we free ourselves from being judged and condemned. When we hold on to unforgiveness, we in essence build a tall, thick wall around the area of our lives where unforgiveness dwells. We hold on to bitterness, which causes even more trouble (Heb. 12:15), and exclude God from manifesting His forgiveness upon us in that area, granting access to the spirit of condemnation, resentment, and hate.

Think of it this way: When someone shines a light on a sealed, dark building, the light can only come into the building where windows and doors are open. If none are open, as much as the light may shine around the house, there is no way the light may enter. God's mercy and forgiveness are like that light. If we close off walls of unforgiveness, God's mercy and forgiveness cannot penetrate fully into our lives.

When that happens, judgment and condemnation—instead of Jesus—take over and reign in us. Have you ever heard of a person adamantly saying, "I'm never going to be an alcoholic like my father or mother," just to watch that person become the very thing he or she judged and condemned—an alcoholic? That's because unforgiveness locked the person behind impenetrable walls and locked out God's grace in that area. That person can only be free by forgiving, releasing judgment, and speaking blessing rather than condemnation over his or her enemies.

> Forgiveness isn't designed to favor the forgiven but to bring freedom and healing to the forgiver.

"GIVE"

When the Bible says, "Give, and it will be given to you," it not only refers to the good but also the bad. The more we practice grace, mercy, and forgiveness, the more we welcome them to be multiplied in our lives. Similarly the more we give in to bitterness and unforgiveness, the more we open ourselves up for them to take over our lives. Whatever we sow, we also reap (Gal. 6:7), and the more we sow it, the more we will reap it (2 Cor. 9:6). If you give hate, you will reap it back somehow. Likewise if you give mercy, grace, and forgiveness, you will certainly receive them in return in abundance.

SOUL "SURGERY"

Since the soul can be wounded, and, as with physical wounds, infected, unattended wounds of the soul and deep-lodged traumas need to be repaired. I like to call the process of repair "surgery of the soul." It's something only God can do. Sometimes He does it through supernatural encounters in His presence, and sometimes He uses a person or group of people to help heal those wounds.

When my moment of truth came and I chose to turn my life around and follow God, it was especially hard dealing with my past. I fought each day with a sense of guilt and shame for all the bad things I had done. I knew that God forgave me, but the hardest part was letting go and forgiving myself.

In the midst of understanding that, God took it further. I believe that when the Holy Spirit reminded me of the terrible experiences with molestation as a child, it was so I could surrender it to Him for Him to be able to remove it from my soul. It was also so He could perform an extraordinary act of inner healing that I could not have gone through on my own.

I desperately needed help dislodging the big, rotting stake of hurt and unforgiveness from my heart. It was crippling my ability to be closer to God, be who He made me to be, and be how He made me to be. I needed to place myself, surrender myself, into the expert hands of God. Had I not done so, I wouldn't have experienced any of the freedom I now walk in.

The first step to letting God operate on your soul is to admit and acknowledge that there is an issue and that you need help. In her book *Emerging With Wings: A True Story of Lies, Pain, and the Love That Heals*, Danielle Bernock says it so beautifully: "Trauma is personal. It does not disappear if it is not validated. When it is ignored or invalidated the silent screams continue internally heard only by the one held captive."[6]

Reliving pain, especially pain that we've tried to tuck away, is difficult. Yet, as with a physically infected wound, it will continue to fester and hurt unless we undergo a procedure to heal it. These procedures are often painful, but the good part is once we let Jesus Christ, our heavenly Doctor, heal it, we need not suffer the pain of it again.

Another aspect of soul surgery that we must consider is proper "therapy" time. I'm sure we've all heard of people who have been in terrible accidents and suffered injuries requiring physical therapy to heal properly. During the process of therapy some of them walk different, have problems keeping a healthy pace, and even have great difficulty making little movements. Yet all their progress, though steps may seem small, is reason for celebration. Why? The reason is simply because the outcome of their accidents could have been much worse.

Soul therapy is what comes after soul surgery; it is the process of upkeep and healing within the newly transformed areas. Of course, as with a patient undergoing therapy it takes time, more for some than for others. During that time is when we feed off of the Word of God, our intimate communion with Him, and the implementation of good and renewed thoughts.

When someone has just been through an extreme period of inner healing, we should never expect her to hit the ground running, so to speak. We should, instead, expect her to take baby steps into wholeness, allowing for her to be imperfect and learn at her own pace with the Lord. There is absolutely no problem with being imperfect when learning to walk righteously in newly healed areas of our lives.

Joyce Meyer says, "We don't think there's something wrong with one-year-old children because they can't walk perfectly. They fall down frequently, but we pick them up, love them, bandage them if necessary, and keep working with them. Surely our heavenly Father can do even more for us than we do for our children."[7] In the same way, we must extend grace to those who are learning how to walk with God in new areas of their lives, or, as the Bible says in Galatians 6:1, "restore such a one in a spirit of gentleness."

Mind "Surgery"

In my journey with the Lord I've found that one of the biggest detriments to maintaining a pure lifestyle is my mind. If I stray from thinking thoughts that draw me closer to God and instead persist in a negative mind-set, I feel that mind-set is a detriment to my communion with the Holy Spirit. A passage that I've learned to hold near and dear is Romans 12:2: "Do not be conformed to this world, but be transformed by the renewing of your mind, that you may prove what is the good and acceptable and perfect will of God" (MEV). When my thought process strays from the will of God, so do I. Or as Proverbs 23:7 puts it, "For as he thinks in his heart, so is he."

One of my favorite teachers on this subject is Dr. Caroline Leaf, a neuroscientist who's devoted her life to researching the human brain. Her findings establish how science validates the Word of God. In her book *Switch on Your Brain* she gives in-depth explanations about the effects of our thought processes on our bodies, souls, and spirits. She has found evidence of thoughts forming physical matter in the body; our directed positive thoughts help build a healthier body, but negative thoughts cause our health to decline.

Dr. Leaf says it is our minds that control our bodies; it isn't the other way around. "Matter does not control us; we control matter through our thinking and choosing. We cannot control the events and circumstances of life, but we can control our reactions." [8] She also states that when it comes to living a healthy lifestyle and even healing our thought patterns, we cocreate our destiny together with God, and "God leads, but we have to choose to let God lead." [9] By doing this—adopting good thought patterns and focusing on true, noble, just, pure, lovely, of good report, virtuous, and praiseworthy things (Phil. 4:8)—we in essence become our own microsurgeons by changing the circuitry of our brains through thought. Here's a brilliant quote about that, which blew my mind:

> Our choices—the natural consequences of our thoughts
> and imagination—get "under the skin" of our DNA and
> can turn certain genes on and off, changing the structure
> of the neurons in our brains. So our thoughts, imagina-
> tion, and choices can change the structure and function
> of our brains on every level: molecular, genetic, epigen-
> etic, cellular, structural, neurochemical, electromagnetic,
> and even subatomic. Through our thoughts, we can be
> our own brain surgeons as we make choices that change
> the circuits in our brains. We are designed to do our
> own brain surgery.[10]

She further expounds that this creation of genetic mate-
rial formed by our thoughts is passed on through our DNA,
impacting the next four generations. In the same way we affect
those who come after us, we are directly affected by the repeti-
tive thought patterns—and the actions causing them—that our
ancestors adopted all the way to our great-great-grandparents!
That is certainly an eye-opening fact.

Knowing this, we can see there is a greater level of responsibility on each of us to draw closer to God by renewing our minds,
focusing on God, His Word, and His will for our lives not only
for ourselves but for those who come later in our lineage.

You may ask, "How can I fix my thoughts?" The answer is
simple. We must focus our thoughts on Jesus, pray, reflect, and
hold fast to Scripture. Every time we feel a bad thought coming,
we must bring "every thought into captivity to the obedience of
Christ" (2 Cor. 10:5) and pray, asking God to fill our minds with
His presence. Additionally the best way to have an abundance
of good, pure thoughts is to read and study the Bible on a regular basis. When I'm struggling to keep my mind thinking right
thoughts, the Holy Spirit will bring to my attention the perfect
verse to help me focus on what is right. By catching our thoughts
and submitting them to Jesus, we can settle our spirits to be in
tune with the voice of God.

Lastly, to keep your thoughts right, stay away from things that fuel your bad thoughts. If you are going through a restoration process, steer clear of the people, things, habits, and places that can make you prone to falling again. For instance, if you are being restored from an addiction to pornography, don't go on websites or TV channels that have that kind of content—or better, block those sites and channels altogether. As another example, if you are being healed from drug addiction or alcoholism, don't visit the places or people that enable you to partake, but rather make it a point to spend that time seeking God, praying, and soaking in the Word.

There is no better place to be than in the presence of God. When we draw near to Him, He draws near to us (James 4:8). The key to our restoration and inner healing is to stay close to God, acknowledging that we are weak and He is strong and only He can help us be whole again, if we choose to let Him.

PRAYER FOR RESTORATION

If you are walking through your own journey of restoration and inner healing, know that you are not alone. We live in a broken world, full of pain and suffering, and we are not immune from their effects on our souls. As I walk my own ongoing journey back to wholeness, it is my earnest prayer that you find your place beside Jesus and walk with Him, dependent on Him in your own voyage.

As you go through the tough areas of your restoration process, I encourage you to pray like this:

> *Dear God,*
>
> *I come before You humbly, knowing that You are the strong God, the only One who can make me whole again. I've been through some hard times. These have caused me to think and act in ways that I shouldn't. I cry out to You, knowing I cannot be healed on my own. So I ask You to come now with Your Holy Spirit and begin a work of healing in my soul. I surrender my heart and soul to You so You can heal me and restore me back to the person You always intended for me to be. I trust You, and therefore I willingly abandon myself to Your hands so You can operate a good work in my soul. Remove what is hindering me from being closer to You, and add what I need to be the best version You envisioned of me. I thank You, God, for Your unconditional love and kindness toward me. I praise You for the work You have already begun in me, which I know You will finish as I allow You to.*
>
> *In the name of Jesus I pray, amen.*

PRAYER FOR FORGIVENESS

As you read in this chapter, a big part of restoring our souls is learning how to forgive. Therefore I felt strongly about including a second prayer in this chapter, one that guides us through the proper and biblical way to forgive.

If you are struggling with pain resulting from someone hurting you, there is a way out of that pain: forgiveness. Remember that forgiveness is not designed to benefit the person being forgiven but to bring freedom to the person forgiving. If you forgive, the person with the most to gain is you, not your aggressors. I've experienced greater levels of personal freedom through forgiveness, and I want you to experience that freedom too.

If you need to forgive someone and finally close the chapter on the past and the pain from that wound, I encourage you to pray this prayer out loud (and do so whenever you remember someone who has hurt you whom you need to forgive):

> *Dear God,*
>
> *I come humbling myself before You. I've carried this pain from my past for way too long, and today I want to be free. So I am ready to forgive, as Jesus did me on the cross.*
>
> *Today I choose to forgive (names of the people who have hurt you) for the pain they caused me when they (acts committed).*
>
> *I renounce the lie that because of those people I cannot move forward or live freely. I renounce the lie that I am less because of these wounds. I surrender my pain at the foot of the cross.*
>
> *Today I release (names of the people who have hurt you) from any and all judgment and condemnation that I may have placed upon them. And just as You blessed me when I didn't deserve it, I speak blessing to them and their descendants. I forfeit any curse that I may have said aimed at them and call down blessings from heaven to cover them, that they might find You too.*
>
> *Finally I declare my freedom and make it known in the spiritual realm. Any legal ground the enemy had over me is now canceled by the blood of Jesus because I have forgiven, and I am now forgiven. I break down the walls that I have built around this area of my life by withholding forgiveness. I cast out any spirit of darkness that may have been clinging*

*to my life because of this, and I close every spiritual door
that my unforgiveness caused to be opened.*

In Jesus's name I am free, amen.

SCRIPTURES TO HOLD ON TO

O LORD my God, I cried to you for help, and you have
healed me.

—PSALM 30:2, ESV

Many are the afflictions of the righteous, but the LORD
delivers him out of them all.

—PSALM 34:19, MEV

Bring me out of prison, that I may give thanks to your
name! The righteous will surround me, for you will deal
bountifully with me.

—PSALM 142:7, ESV

He heals the brokenhearted and binds up their wounds.

—PSALM 147:3, NIV

And you shall know the truth, and the truth shall make
you free.

—JOHN 8:32

Part IV

———◆———

∽ DAUGHTER SENT ∽

Chapter 9

∽ HE IS MY FATHER ∽

...for love of Thee, my Father, supremely good, Beauty of all things beautiful.[1]

—AURELIUS AUGUSTINE (354–430 CE)
PHILOSOPHER, THEOLOGIAN, AUTHOR,
AND A THEOLOGICAL FATHER OF THE
REFORMATION AND WESTERN CHRISTIANITY

O NE DAY NEARLY two years into our marriage, Carlos felt moved by the Holy Spirit to bring up the subject of my father. "Babe," he said, "why don't you write a song for your father? I think the Lord wants you to." I looked at him, a little self-conscious, and said, "Huh. Yeah, sure. That sounds nice. I'll do it one of these days," and left it at that. Two weeks went by, and he felt the nudge of the Spirit again. So he asked me: "Honey, have you written anything for your father yet? How's your song coming along?" With a serious look on my face I replied, "I've been really busy. I'll get to it when I get to it." He shrugged, signaling OK, and walked away. A few weeks later he heard God speak to him about it again, so he asked me, "Babe, did you write that song for your dad yet?" Hearing the question again made my blood boil, and my wrath erupted: "Didn't I tell you I'd get to it? Well, I haven't, and this is just too much pressure. Stop pressuring me! Why can't you just leave it alone? Just let what's dead stay dead!"

His face became pale and froze in shock. I'd never reacted like that without provocation. The ancient pain of my father's death had been embedded in my heart for so long that I'd forgotten it was there. Carlos just said, "Sorry," and went into another room. My thoughts rushed in my agony; I couldn't silence my train of thought. This invitation to honor my father with a song had stirred up the dirt at the bottom of the stagnant waters of my soul, and it stank.

That night I was watching a rerun of *ER*, my favorite TV show at the time. That particular episode depicted the story of a man with a troubled past who had become an alcoholic and was dying of liver failure due to cirrhosis. Every aspect of that character's life reminded me of my father. Seeing that man die in the film, I felt as if I were watching my father go through it right before my eyes. In the last scene the man sees himself in an alternate reality with his son and tells him, "I'm so sorry; I'm so sorry," and his last words are, "It's OK... son." Those words pierced me. I didn't have a chance to say good-bye to my daddy. His life just slipped away from me, and that chapter of my life had remained open, without conclusion, all those years. The sharp pain I'd carried since the day he died still cut through my soul.

Seeing that character lying lifeless on the hospital bed made me break down. I cried what my six-year-old self could not cry when life changed so fast, demanding that I grow up all too soon. Broken, I couldn't even hold my head up. Immediately at hearing my sobbing, Carlos rushed in from the other room. He'd been listening and waiting. He knew from the Holy Spirit that a work was being done in me. He scooped me up in his big, warm arms and simply held me as I wailed. After a while, when my crying had begun to subside, he asked with such tenderness, "My love, do you need to go say good-bye to your dad?"

I hadn't realized that for all those years, I had been not only suffering the loss but also grieving never having said good-bye to the most important man in my life. But the Holy Spirit was up to something. For weeks He'd been bringing all that pain to the surface to heal it. And my answer to Carlos's sweet question was a shaky and quivering *yes* as both Carlos and the Holy Spirit engulfed me and remained still with me in my suffering.

After several months, the time had come for our trip to upstate New York. It was a stretch for us in every sense of the word. We lived on a minimal salary, so we invested what little savings we had so I could take this step toward healing. We went to see my grandmother, whom I had not seen since a few days before Daddy passed. During the eighteen years that followed, my relationship with my grandmother had consisted only of occasional letters and birthday and holiday cards.

The moment we saw each other, it was like seeing Dad again. Maybe it was because she was the green-eyed matriarch who had passed down her beautiful eyes to me through him, but I could see him in her gaze, and I knew she could see him in mine. It was bittersweet. The air felt sad, perhaps because he couldn't be there to witness this beautiful moment. Despite the slight heartache I knew we were both feeling, Grandma and I fell in love with each other all over again. Our initial icebreakers led us into a formal and somewhat shy conversation, but soon it turned into a long-overdue and quite endearing heart-to-heart exchange.

Later that day Grandpa took me to Daddy's grave site. When we arrived at the cemetery, I thought it would be as in the movies. I had visualized myself walking through aisles of gravestones, having a few minutes to prepare for the fateful moment that lay ahead. However, much to my surprise, when I opened the car door, I could quickly glance over a small-town graveyard. And there it was, not many steps away—my family name on a large black marble tombstone. As I took my first step, my knees weakened. The sting inside me swelled, just like that moment Mom came down from Dad's hospital room with the

> I was in no rush to come out of my moment of mourning; God understood and made sure I was comforted in my hurt.

news of his death. It had been almost eighteen years, but the sting was just as bad. In that regard it felt as if not a day had passed.

With each step my shoulders felt a thousand pounds heavier. My pace became slower and weaker until I collapsed right in front of his headstone. I wanted to run away, but at the same time I wanted to stay. In some strange way I wanted to reach down into the ground and wake him up so I could feel him hold me again. The pain was agonizing, and I bawled. I cried out his name. I let my head fall to the ground as I wept.

I was left to have a moment alone. Then it was just me before that tombstone. I had to finally let him go. But how? I didn't know how. Suddenly I could feel a breeze sweep over me, blowing my hair from my tear-ridden face. I could feel an embrace that was deeper than what any human could offer. It was the Holy Spirit. He was there in my pain and stayed as long as I needed him to. I was in no rush to come out of my moment of mourning; God understood and made sure I was comforted in my hurt.

> I realized my identity was no longer based on my fatherlessness.

After crying for a while and letting all the years of suffering out of my heart, I felt the Holy Spirit guide me in what to say and do. Under His direction I spoke to my father. "Daddy, I'm mad at you. You left me! You didn't think that your addiction would hurt me, but it did. I've had to live all these years in pain because of you. How I've missed you, needed you, and resented you. But today I forgive you. I release you from all my judgments, and I let go of you. I'm finally going to bury you now. I declare I am now free from this grief in the name of Jesus Christ. And I hold the hope that someday, when it's my time, I'll see you again. I love you, and I'll always miss you. But now it's time to say good-bye."

That day it was my heart that could finally rest in peace. While I returned home from that divinely appointed trip, I realized my identity was no longer based on my fatherlessness; my existence no longer revolved around my pain and what I'd lost. My identity was now found in the One who lifted me from orphaned knees and gave me a home, a meaning, and a purpose. He carried me through my hurt, toward healing, and back to wholeness in Him. God had now become my Father and my all.

Just a few days later I wrote my daddy a song. It was finished within minutes, and I titled it "The Day That You Went Home." With the flow of the melody I could feel God putting in the last suture in the repair He'd just made to my heart. It was like medicine to my soul. This song wasn't intended to be on a record or sung around the world; this one was for my daddy, for me, and for our perfect Father, who now filled my every void.

WHO IS MY FATHER?

For years I tried to imagine who my father was as a man. The only perception I had of him was whatever conjectures my childhood mind could form. To me he was the sweetest, kindest, funniest, greatest person in this world. To this day I am impressed by the big, tender heart he had; I haven't met anyone quite so empathic, sensitive, and deep-loving as he was.

However, I grew older and started to process things more like an adult, able to see how adults tend to mask the bad and magnify the good within themselves for the sake of their children. Then I began to wonder, "Was he really that loving? Was I really as important to him as he made it seem when we were together?" If so, why couldn't he just put down the bottle and still be here? In my adolescence the wide-eyed wonder I'd held in my heart for my dad began to cloud into resentment, and later bitterness, resulting in rebellion. I began to see God from my twisted perception of what it meant to be a father.

I started blaming God for taking my dad so early, for not performing some divine intervention to supernaturally end my father's addiction. During that time I began judging my father as being a good-for-nothing alcoholic who couldn't even keep himself alive to be a father. I also unknowingly began to judge God, believing that, like my father, He was incompetent to father me.

When we see God as Father, we have a human inclination to measure Him according to our earthly father's example. In other words, if our dads were or are good, loving fathers, then we have a better idea of how good Father God is. But if our dads were or are irritable, blunt, mistreating, abusive, violent, or absent, then we think that is how God must be. In my case, my father was a loving, yet flawed, individual and ultimately was absent from my life.

Whenever I heard of God being my Father, I simply couldn't see anything more than this huge figure who was the Creator of everything, almighty, and all-powerful, and who loved me but was just too far away. I believed deep down inside that, like my father, who had already passed, God was in heaven reigning over the big and relevant things of creation. I most certainly did not consider myself one of those relevant things that merited God's attention. I also thought that if I was a good girl in this life, I'd be able to go to heaven when I die and only then get to know God, have a relationship with Him, and enjoy Him.

How mistaken I was. God is not far at all. He's as close as our own breath; He *is* that breath. "The LORD God formed man of the dust of the ground, and breathed into his nostrils the breath of life; and man became a living being" (Gen. 2:7). He's the Alpha and the Omega—the Beginning and the End—the wielder of time and space, and the Master of all things impossible. At the same time He's that Daddy that still makes time to embrace His children in His great and perfect arms!

The Bible is full of characteristics of God the Father. He is Love (1 John 4:8) and loves us abundantly, persistently, and lavishly (1 John 3:1; Jeremiah 31:3). He is forever compassionate (Ps. 103:13), even to the ones who are challenging to Him (Isa. 49:13–16). Not only is He the Father of compassion, but He is also the God of comfort (2 Cor. 1:3). He is loyal through and through and until the end (Isa. 43:2). He's nurturing and cares for our needs (Deut. 1:31).

God is familiar and warm in His affections; He loves to be called Abba—an endearing word for *Father*[2] (Gal. 4:6). He is perfect (Matt. 5:48), His ways and protection of us are perfect (Ps. 18:30), and therefore He is incapable of failing as an earthly father would. He loves to give (James 1:17; Matt. 7:11), so much so that He gave Jesus to save us and have us by His side for eternity (John 3:16).

Our heavenly Father is our Protector (2 Sam. 22:3–4; Ps. 46:1; 91:1–3; 121:7–8; 2 Tim. 4:18). He takes care of those who are neglected, weak, and defenseless (Ps. 68:5). He is an everlasting Father (Isa. 9:6), always there when we need Him. He corrects and disciplines us when necessary (Heb. 12:7, 10), yet is ever forgiving (1 John 1:9). And most importantly God *never* leaves us (Matt. 28:20).

We have the grandest Father of all. He loves us profusely, guides us wisely, and is absolute in His pursuit of us. He never grows weary of us, but His passion toward us is unwavering. He does not tire of blessing us abundantly and longs for us to live the best and most fulfilled life in Him. His utmost desire since the beginning of the foundation of the earth is *us*! Even when our earthly parents fall short in their responsibility to raise us well, we still have the best Father in God. All we need to do is let Him be who He is best: our Dad.

PRAYER TO GOD OUR FATHER

I've come to know God as a Father as I've allowed Him to become my all. At first it was not easy to give up control and simply let God take the reins of my life. Yet the more I surrendered to Him, the more He would reveal Himself to me. In that process I came to love Him more than I could have ever imagined.

If you've had a hard time with father figures, I know it's not easy to remove your conceptions of what a father is. But I tell you, God is the perfect Father you've always desired, needed, and dreamed of. The best part is He is real, and He is there. He waits for you to surrender and let Him in, truly and fully.

I pray that you may know God the Father as I have—and even more. I encourage you to pursue and get to know the Father's heart and pray this prayer:

> Father God,
>   You who are in heaven reigning over all, I praise You. I come before You thirsty for Your love. Today I choose to acknowledge You as my Father. Forgive me if I have judged You according to my earthly parents' mistakes. I know now that You are perfect, all-loving, compassionate, kind, nurturing, protecting, encouraging, loyal, and the greatest Giver of good things. You are real and intensely pursuant of me, and I want to be intensely pursuant of You. As I surrender to You, come fill my heart, even in the areas where I've been holding back. Come take over my life and teach me how to obey and follow Your will. Today I will lift my head up high because You are my Father and I am Your child.
>   Amen.

Scriptures to Hold On To

Yet for us there is one God, the Father, of whom are all things, and we for Him; and one Lord Jesus Christ, through whom are all things, and through whom we live.
—1 Corinthians 8:6

Blessed be the God and Father of our Lord Jesus Christ, who has blessed us with every spiritual blessing in the heavenly places in Christ.
—Ephesians 1:3, mev

But now, O Lord, You are our Father; we are the clay, and You are our potter; and we all are the work of Your hand.
—Isaiah 64:8, mev

That you may be sons of your Father in heaven; for He makes His sun rise on the evil and on the good, and sends rain on the just and on the unjust.
—Matthew 5:45

Therefore do not be like them. For your Father knows the things you have need of before you ask Him.
—Matthew 6:8

Look at the birds of the air, for they neither sow nor reap nor gather into barns; yet your heavenly Father feeds them. Are you not of more value than they?
—Matthew 6:26

If you then, being evil, know how to give good gifts to your children, how much more will your Father who is in heaven give good things to those who ask Him!
—Matthew 7:11, mev

Chapter 10

∽ I AM HIS CHILD ∽

I'm no longer a slave to fear, I am a child of God.[1]

—"No Longer Slaves," by Jonathan David
and Melissa Helser

To call yourself a child of God is one thing. To be called
a child of God by those who watch your life is another
thing altogether.[2]

—Max Lucado
Best-Selling Author,
Preacher, and Pastor

O**n the day** I set out to write this book, I came to
the realization of who I really am in the eyes of God.
Spring had fully bloomed in Miami, Florida. I was part
of a literature and music expo. I had been attending this annual
event for a decade, since the beginning of my music career and
ministry. Yet this year was special. It was a year in which God
was fulfilling specific promises, just as He said He would. One of
them was that I'd become an author.

One particular day during this event I was scheduled to meet
the publisher of this book first thing in the morning to sign our
contract. As I walked toward the meeting room, my heart beat
louder, my steps grew lighter, and my smile expanded as wide as
my face could hold. When all documents were finalized, my husband, Carlos, and I celebrated with our new literary family and
went about our busy schedule for the day. What a jam-packed,

hectic day lay ahead! With multiple radio interviews, television appearances, musical performances, and many meet and greets with conference attendees who love and support our ministry, morning soon turned into evening.

My last commitment of the day was to lead worship onstage during a late-night concert. However, some last-minute production emergencies set the schedule back a couple of hours. There I was, thankful for such a productive and blessed day, but drained and exhausted after being on my feet since the predawn hours of the morning. I was about to hit the twenty-hours-on-the-run mark of my day, powered at that point by pure stamina.

On a typical day I would take time to pause, allowing me to take a breath and talk to God. Sometimes I'll have much to say. Sometimes I'll just make small talk with Him. Other times I simply bask in the warmth of His presence and don't say a word. I'm so in love with my Savior that the important thing for me in those moments is just to exchange my love with Him. I've come to depend on God so much that I often find myself desperately seeking more time with Him than merely morning and evening prayers. This particular day became such a whirlwind that I didn't have that time to talk to my heavenly Father throughout the day. So when I heard of the last-minute delay in the stage schedule, I saw the perfect opportunity to connect with my Abba, even if for only a few minutes.

I found myself in a corner talking to my Abba. Letting out a tired sigh, I whispered, "Thank You, Lord." In an instant, before saying anything else, I could feel His oh-so-overwhelming glory embracing every bit of my existence. And in that moment He gave me a vision. I've been blessed with being able to see visions from God; I've seen many since I was a child. But this one was different because for the first time it was a vision of me! I was startled, as I was used to seeing visions of other people and their situations, not of myself.

In the vision I could see what looked like snapshots of myself throughout that very long day. I did not see myself from my own perspective but from one of a much taller person, watching me from above. As I looked down, I saw myself in the morning talking to God, getting ready for my day, at my meeting signing the contract, at every radio and television interview, hugging people, taking pictures and signing autographs with whoever asked for one, prepping backstage, and finally in that very moment in the corner talking to God. Curiosity about what God wanted to reveal to me pressed me further into His presence. He whispered back to me with the sweetest voice ever to exist in and beyond creation. I could even sense Him smiling as He said to me, "I delight in you!"

I was completely shaken by such a statement. Soon after, it was time to take the platform. I determined to keep my composure and fulfill my last commitment of the day, but I longed to continue this conversation with God. So when I was done, I made my way to my hotel room in haste. When I got to my room, I decompressed my soul from such a wound-up day, finally slipping into bed to resume my precious chat with God. I began to thank Him again, astonished that God—the sovereign, eternal God, the Creator of the heavens and the earth, the most high King, of greatest power, worthy of all honor and glory forever—would tell little ole me that He delights in me. I could hardly believe it! Nor could I understand it.

I knew He didn't give me this vision because I'm hyper-spiritual or anything of the type. Neither did He speak to me that way because I deserve it, because sincerely I do not. He gave it to me, as He has many others, simply because He wanted to say something to me. God has a particular way of coming down to our level; like the Dad He is, He kneels to see us eye-to-eye and speak to us in ways we best understand. Often if we are visually driven, He'll give us a picture or a visual. If we're auditory, we may hear a sound or words spoken inside of us. If we're sensory, we may smell or feel something in our bodies. That day God spoke to me through a vision and those four sweet words, "I delight in you."

As I thanked and praised God, I could feel the Holy Spirit bring to my memory the passages in Matthew 3:17 and 17:5: "This is My beloved Son, in whom I am well pleased." He impressed on my heart to

> Being certain of God's fatherhood of us is only part of our knowledge of Him; the rest is knowing, accepting, and embracing that we are also His children!

look up the literal translation in the Bible, which said, "This is My Son—the Beloved, in whom I did delight" (YLT). I could not conceive that God would say those words to *me*. All my life I thought they were exclusively for Jesus.

As all these thoughts flooded my mind, I tried to get a good grip of this new realization, and I heard the Father whisper to me again, "I am your Father." Then He paused before going on to say, "But you are also *My* child!" Those words reverberated so loudly in my spirit that I began to weep. Even now as I remember this, I shake and my eyes well up with tears. I could finally understand. Knowing He is my Father is not enough to make me whole. Being certain of God's fatherhood of us is only part of our knowledge of Him; the rest is knowing, accepting, and embracing that we are also His children!

CHILDREN OF GOD

I'm sure most people have heard the term *God, the Father*, which I discussed in greater detail in the previous chapter. I'm also certain that most people have understood the term *children of God* referring to Christians. But do we really know what being a child of God is? Let's see.

The word *child* refers to many things, but in this connotation it is son or daughter, which means a "person in relation to his [or her] parents by birth, adoption, or marriage."³ In modern-day society the notion of being a child of someone seems to be in decline. It is not rare to see children grow older, only to stray, as if to escape from their parents. It may well be for a good reason, such as neglect or abuse. Yet some try hard to distance themselves from their fathers and mothers over disagreements that are much simpler than they may seem. Some even feel embarrassed by who their progenitors are.

Please understand that I am not judging in any way. I'm simply pointing it out because for a season I was one of those distanced children. In my rebellion I did everything I could to reject my mother and her wisdom as well as close the door to any relationship with my stepfather. At times I would embrace confrontation more than a civilized talk. I was so unhappy with myself that I cast off anything that related to my formation, which for a time represented painful memories for me. Constantly looking through the veil of my broken understanding, I could not see the truth that I was not what my family had made me, but I was, in fact, the person God intended me to be. Now I can see through the restoration of my thinking that the Lord used each and every one of my circumstances to form me into who He wanted me to become: His.

So you may ask yourself: "What does it mean to be children of God? Is it the same as knowing and accepting that God is our Father?" Absolutely not. Here's why. Many of us acknowledge God as our Father and Creator. A great many of us are even reverent when speaking about God or going to church, or even when someone else is praying to the Father. But living up to being His child, truly living as His child, though immediately related, is quite different.

To Be a Child

The first thing we must understand is that to be a child of God, we must emphasize being like a *child*. The Bible tells a story of how one day Jesus's disciples were rebuking people for bringing children to Jesus for Him to place His hands upon and pray. He immediately responded and "called them to Him and said, 'Let the little children come to Me, and do not forbid them; for of such is the kingdom of God. Assuredly, I say to you, whoever does not receive the kingdom of God as a little child will by no means enter it'" (Luke 18:16–17).

Have you ever observed a child? Have you ever looked closely at how a child acts when he believes in something? I certainly have. I love children, and I learn so much from them. What I've learned most about them is their belief. The faith of children is unwavering. They stick to what they believe is true and claim that belief whenever possible. If a child in a healthy relationship with a parent sees his parent's hands extended to catch him, he does not hesitate to jump. Furthermore, he *expects* to be safe with his mommy and daddy. If his parents make a promise, he knows that promise will come to pass; if not, he sure knows how to remind them enough to ensure that his promises will be fulfilled. Children know in whom they believe.

> Constantly looking through the veil of my broken understanding, I could not see the truth that I was not what my family had made me, but I was, in fact, the person God intended me to be.

A true child of God knows it is absolutely OK to depend on Him. We were designed to be dependent on God, not independent, as this world has fought for millennia to make us believe. Everything we are, everything we do, and everything we will be able to do is because of Him. We *need* God; therefore we must depend on Him as the only Source of life.

Personally, a good example of this is my relocation. Shortly after my getting married and having spent most of my life in Puerto Rico, God spoke to Carlos and me about moving away from the island. It was initially difficult to obey with childlike faith. It was so hard that we hesitated, waiting an entire year before taking a leap of faith and deciding to believe God's promises. That was probably one of the hardest years of my life.

Having experienced stability and beginning to see our ministry grow, all of a sudden we started going through an abrupt season of scarcity. It was as if the faucet of our blessing had turned and our source had been closed off tight. Upon reaching the end of a year since God had spoken to us, we understood why we were going through this season of drought. We learned that when you enter into a covenant of obedience with God, He takes it seriously. When He says to move, it's because there is a greater blessing that emerges as fruit of our obedience. We also learned that when God speaks about moving, especially relocating, He moves out blessings to the place where we *should* be and not necessarily where we *want* to be.

When we finally understood that our obedience and dependence on God are our greatest blessings, we gathered whatever money we had left and bought two one-way airline tickets, and we filled four suitcases with clothing and two boxes with our most important documents. We gave away everything else. And we started over, taking our first big leap of faith as a family. We moved to the US mainland, to Orlando, Florida.

We lived through a desert season in which God processed us, detoxing us of self-dependence and nurturing us with a newfound dependence on Him. Six years later, when God asked us to move again, this time to Dallas, Texas—where we currently reside—it was less difficult to obey, for we already knew that when the Father says "jump," it's because His arms are there ready to catch us, sustain us, and carry us to a better place. Why? It's simple: because "where the Spirit of the Lord is" [and I like to also say "where we allow ourselves to be guided to where the Spirit of the Lord is"], "there is liberty [or "freedom," as the NIV puts it]," and "we...are being transformed into [His] image from glory to glory...by the Spirit of the Lord" (2 Cor. 3:17–18).

In order to depend on God and fulfill our destinies in Him,

we must have the unshakable faith of a child—the kind of faith
that will look at the mountain God said He'd remove and say,
"Move out of my way, big mountain; my Daddy said so!"; the kind
of faith that will not falter in the storm but will remain close to
the Father to weather it under His big arms, knowing that in due
time God will surely do what He said He will do; the kind of
faith without which it is "impossible to please Him" (Heb. 11:6);
and as I like to add, the kind of bold faith that makes our Father
giggle in awe at how strongly we believe Him.

To Be *His* Child

Aside from being *like* children, there's also the matter of living
our lives in a way that identifies us as *God's* children. Though
they seem similar and go hand in hand, the latter is much more
than the former. In a great book titled *Think Differently, Live
Differently: Keys to a Life of Freedom*, author Bob Hamp depicts
a brilliant story that exemplifies this very notion. It's called "The
Parable of the Acrobat." A baby boy was born to an amazing
couple of acrobats. Their ability to defy gravity and show super-
human abilities had been passed on for generations. So when the
child was born, there was indeed the promise that he'd be just
that, a phenomenally talented acrobat.

His birth was nothing short of a great, joyous celebration, for
there was another generation to carry forth the marvels of these
remarkable tumblers. Shortly after his birth they were all on their
way to the next destination, where they would hold their usual
awe-inspiring shows. Several hours into their trip they realized
that somehow the newborn child had fallen off their wagon. The
desperate parents and friends doubled back to try to find the baby,
expecting the worst, but to no avail. The child was nowhere to
be found.

Shortly before the acrobats had completed scanning the areas
where they had already traveled, a farming couple in a nearby
town were out walking. Their stroll was interrupted by an unusual

sound in the brush, which they found to be the tender, little baby who had fallen from the wagon, miraculously intact. They couldn't have children of their own, and their barrenness had slowly but surely taken away any hope of ever having a child, until now.

The farmers took the child in and raised him as their own, teaching him the quiet, steady lifestyle they were used to. But soon he grew fond of adventure and heights and had an urge to defy gravity. He instinctively climbed on everything he could and pirouetted his way up and down obstacles. Everything within him urged him to climb, to hang, to jump, and to do it all over again; his genes dictated his moves more than his upbringing could. This did not sit well with his parents, the ever ground-ridden farmers. Soon the look of sheer terror on his mom's face whenever he gave in to his natural gifts and the spankings he got from his dad whenever he would impulsively give them a scare made him feel there was something very wrong with him.

As years went by, his inner sense of self changed. He slowly lost the hope that he would ever partake in the gravity-defying adventures that truly excited him and made him feel fulfilled. Instead, to be a good son, he resigned himself to the quiet life of a farmer. As the author said:

> In years past, the deep yearnings had been a distraction; now they were not even a memory. He no longer glanced at the hills and trees. He had successfully packed away those feelings like an old set of tools—no longer useful, no longer used....He soon developed a reputation as an angry young man with a penchant for fighting. The pent-up strength in his muscles screamed for an outlet....But after a fight, he never felt relieved, just ashamed. The shame caused him to avoid his peers, and he became increasingly isolated. The isolation led to more frustration, and it became an endless cycle.[4]

One day he unexpectedly saw a poster that intrigued him. Its display of many gravity-defying instruments tugged at his insides in an unexplainable way. He and his parents made plans to go to the show, which was passing through town. When the day came for the show, so did an awakening inside the young man. After the show he was immediately drawn to the amazing gymnast entertainers who had been in the spotlight, wowing the audience.

Among all the young acrobats were two older ones who caught the attention of the farmer and his wife, who had kept close to their boy. The acrobat woman noticed how closely the farmer woman watched the young man and asked her if he was her son. That ice-breaking question evolved into a much deeper conversation. Soon after answering affirmatively, the farmer's wife asked the acrobats, "You have children?" The answer prompted the sad story of how they had lost their baby, who had fallen off their wagon so many years ago. After hearing the details of the story, it was inevitable the farmers would realize the truth about the child they'd kept for so long. Immediately they felt compelled to tell them that this boy, their son, was truly the acrobats' lost son.

When the young man had finished chatting with the other acrobats, he came over to his parents. He couldn't help but notice the emotional heaviness between them and the two other adults standing close by. He was compelled to ask what was going on. All the adults proceeded to take turns telling him the story of who he was and how he got where he was. A whirlwind of thoughts rushed to his mind, and everything was beginning to make sense to him—his urges, his dreams, his desires, his frustrations…everything. Before the night was over, realizing their lives would never be the same, the farmers gave their boy the option of going with his birth parents, following in their footsteps, and finally being who he was born to be.

Fantastic story, right? Now, if you were in this situation, I'm sure you'd also have many thoughts running through your head. Perhaps you'd even feel empathy for these people who share your eye color and DNA. You may even feel a little resentment toward your adoptive parents for not telling you that you were adopted. But as you try to put yourself in this child's imaginary situation, I ask you, would you immediately feel like, know, walk like, and carry yourself like the acrobats' child? Chances are your answer is *no*.

Physically we start to develop who we will be from a very early age. The same applies to our spiritual growth. From the moment we accept Jesus Christ and surrender our lives to Him, we begin growing in our spiritual identity. Let's go back to the story for a moment as I point a few things out. Imagine that you are the youngster in this story, and you are discovering these things about yourself. The adoptive parents symbolize your upbringing, your hometown customs, or even the spiritual leaders who have surrounded you—perhaps the church family of which you are or have been a part. These things, places, and people have—knowingly or unknowingly—formed you and facilitated your introduction to your real, actual, and true Father, God. The fall from the wagon symbolizes our fall from God's grace due to sin, which satan has always used to keep us immersed in guilt, shame, and frustrations that separate us from God.

Throughout your life, and since the beginning of the foundation of the earth, God has been doing immeasurable things to be reunited with you, to conquer your heart and bring you home to Him. But while you may have discovered that He is indeed your Father and that He sent His Son, Jesus Christ, to pay the ultimate price for your ransom, there is still a processing of thought and spirit that needs to take place to become His child; it's a decision.

This "Parable of the Acrobat" ends with the young man deciding to follow his birth parents, to change his life to learn their ways, and to live according to the truth of his sonship.

The same applies to us all. We are all faced with a similar decision regarding God. We must *choose* to follow God and make adjustments to our lifestyles and thought processes to live according to our true identities as children of God. We must decide to act and think as God's children to live as such.

Here's another way to look at it: You may go to church every week and be involved in the church activities. You may adhere to the church's beliefs and even its dress code. You may recite Bible verses. But when it comes to living your personal life, the life you live when no one is watching you, are you behaving like God's child?

This reminds me of a day when I was doing a late-night sound check before an event I had the next day. During our break I went to the restroom, which was a disaster. The toilet seat was not clean, and someone had splashed water all over the floor and dropped paper on the ground. With the coming and going of hundreds of people that day it had turned into a muddy mess that certainly would require a lot of additional work to clean.

All of a sudden I felt compassion for the cleaning person. I felt I should act on that compassion, and I thought, "Well, maybe I should clean up this mess." I instantly felt my flesh refute me as I heard a whisper in my head: "Now why would I do something like that? Clean up this mess? But there's no one here. Who could I possibly impress?" After a brief pause I rolled up my sleeves anyway, grabbed the roll of paper towels, and began to clean and wipe things up in that solitary public bathroom. Then I could hear the voice of the Holy Spirit say, "Well, I'm here, and you're certainly impressing me." With that I could envision His smile, as if suggesting an "Atta girl."

I don't share this as a perfect example of what a child of God would do. It is far from that. More than focusing on what I was doing, I want you to focus on my heart. It didn't matter that I picked up a roll of paper and cleaned a dirty bathroom. What mattered is I wanted to do what would make God smile. I wanted to serve, not because I was being watched but because I knew that is what would please God. I love the Holy Spirit so much that every day I strive to make Him happy.

Being children of God is not a penned term that prophets and apostles decided would "sound pretty" in the Bible. Being children of God is living, walking, breathing, talking, doing, and abstaining from doing for the sake of pleasing our Father. Thus, we focus on loving the Lord our God with all our hearts, all our souls, all our minds, and all our strength, and loving our neighbor as ourselves, as Christ said in Luke 10:27. So what is our identity as children of God? We are "a chosen generation, a royal priesthood, a holy nation, His own special people, that [we] may proclaim the praises of Him who called [us] out of darkness into His marvelous light; who once were not a people but are now the people of God, who had not obtained mercy but now have obtained mercy" (1 Pet. 2:9–10).

ABBA, I LOVE YOU!

I particularly love to call God *Abba*, which, as I mentioned, means *Father*, in both Aramaic (old Hebrew) and Arabic. However, it's more than just a translation; it is a term of endearment from a beloved child to a beloved Father in a warm, affectionate expression of filial confidence in a dependent relationship. This word does not have a perfect equivalent in any other language,[5] but perhaps our closest word in the English language would be *Daddy*.

I have found that a key to growing in my Father-daughter relationship with God is not only to do His will but also to delight in and take great pleasure in just being with Him. The more I seek Him simply to be with Him, the more I fall in love with His presence. Our true identity as God's children is revealed when we learn to let go of ourselves into His love, His embrace, His will, and His guidance. One of my favorite Scripture passages is Psalm 37:4–6:

> Delight yourself also in the LORD,
> And He shall give you the desires of your heart.
> Commit your way to the LORD,
> Trust also in Him,
> And He shall bring it to pass.

He shall bring forth your righteousness as the light,
And your justice as the noonday.

When we delight in our personal, intimate time with our Abba, we must also trust Him and devote our lifestyles to serving Him and furthering His name. Then we will be given the desires of our hearts, He will make our ways come to pass in perfect fashion, and He will make it known before all others that He is our Father and we are righteous and just *in* Him.

So being a child of God is having simple faith in a God who has never gone back on any of His promises, it is delighting in His presence when no one else can see, it is doing everything we possibly can to please Him simply to make Him smile over us, and it is knowing that in our humanity He is still a forgiving and restoring Father.

PRAYER FROM A CHILD OF
GOD TO THE FATHER

Remember, there's no penance we must do to be God's child. All
we need to do is live for Him by truly setting our hearts on pursuing and pleasing Him. Every day I learn something new about
my relationship with my Father and my identity as His child.
Every day I pray that He helps me understand a little bit more—
and He does. If you want to know more of your identity as a true
child of God, I encourage you to pray a prayer like this:

> *Dear Abba,*
> *I love You. I desire Your presence, and I long to know*
> *more of You. I'm sorry if I thought that my relationship*
> *with You depends on what I do more than on how or for*
> *Whom I do it. Help me delight and take pleasure in the*
> *intimate times we spend together. I pray Deuteronomy 29:4,*
> *that I may have "a heart to perceive and eyes to see and ears*
> *to hear" what You speak to my heart each day. Allow me*
> *to know You more, that I may fall deeper in love with You.*
> *And guide me to be who You want me to be and do what*
> *You want me to do. Abba, I love You. Be my Father, and I*
> *will be Your child.*
> *In Jesus's name I pray and believe, amen.*

SCRIPTURES TO HOLD ON TO

But you are a chosen generation, a royal priesthood, a
holy nation, His own special people, that you may proclaim the praises of Him who called you out of darkness
into His marvelous light; who once were not a people
but are now the people of God, who had not obtained
mercy but now have obtained mercy.

—1 PETER 2:9–10

For I am persuaded that neither death nor life, nor angels nor principalities nor powers, nor things present nor things to come, nor height nor depth, nor any other created thing, shall be able to separate us from the love of God which is in Christ Jesus our Lord.

—ROMANS 8:38–39

But you, when you pray, go into your room, and when you have shut your door, pray to your Father who is in the secret place; and your Father who sees in secret will reward you openly.

—MATTHEW 6:6

For you did not receive the spirit of bondage again to fear, but you received the Spirit of adoption by whom we cry out, "Abba, Father."

—ROMANS 8:15

One God and Father of all, who is above all, and through all, and in us all.

—EPHESIANS 4:6, DRA

Chapter 11

❦ "GO GET MY BABIES" ❦

Go forth today, by the help of God's Spirit, vowing and declaring that in life—come poverty, come wealth, in death—come pain or come what may, you are and ever must be the Lord's. For this is written on your heart, "We love Him because He first loved us." [1]

—CHARLES SPURGEON (1834–1892)
ENGLISH PASTOR AND WRITER, KNOWN
AS THE "PRINCE OF PREACHERS"

I T WAS A warm Friday night in Puerto Rico, and it had been close to three years since having my wonderful encounter of salvation with the Lord. Service at our church had already closed in prayer. Yet for a hungry few this only meant we'd get to have a few more hours of prayer and seeking God without time constraints. We were used to having spontaneous, vigil-like times of prayer, which went into the wee hours of the night as we sought more of God's presence.

During these times we'd see and feel manifestations of the presence of God, which resulted in supernatural healing, deliverance, and even a few signs and wonders, such as what the Bible says Jesus did (Acts 2:22), and which we would also experience in a greater way (John 5:20). Those times were indeed life-giving to my spirit. Each time, I felt something new being healed, unveiled, revealed, and restored inside of me. It was a beautiful environment where a broken soul such as mine was able to continue mending, growing, and flourishing.

That night as we pursued God, He certainly had something special planned. Our youth pastor felt driven to bring a word of knowledge to the remnant of us still there. He said the Holy Spirit was speaking to him, saying He wanted to reveal something to us related to our purpose. I could feel anticipation rise up in my heart as the youth pastor spoke with a tremendous anointing. He said, "The Holy Spirit wants to touch you, some of you even physically, and guide you to an area of the building where He will reveal His purpose and calling for your life." Then he prayed and said: "Lord, come touch us as You're saying You will. You are welcome to do what You want to do. Reveal to us Your purpose. Come now, Holy Spirit!"

I was standing in the middle aisle at the center of the sanctuary. I'd closed my eyes and extended my hands as if to receive something. Suddenly I felt a warm hand grab my right hand. For a second I thought perhaps it was my husband or another of the ushers. As I was on staff at the church and now part of the pastoral family, it wasn't rare to be called upon to help pray and minister to other people during times like these. Yet as I opened my eyes, I was flabbergasted to see no one was beside me! Nevertheless the hand still held on to mine, and it now felt hot as fire.

I could barely hold in my amazement. It was the Holy Spirit! He was touching me, *literally* holding my hand! In the midst of the humbling anticipation within me, I couldn't help but try to guess what would come next. My mind raced in different directions: "Will He take me to the altar, behind the microphone? I am a singer, and I sing in worship here. That's probably it! He's going to talk to me about my music!" I braced myself to be moved forward to the platform, but to my surprise the hand started pulling me backward, tugging me toward the entrance.

I was walking backward without really being able to see where I was going; I only knew I was not headed where I thought I'd be going. As I passed the auditorium doors, I saw the church offices doorway and thought, "Ah, OK. He's going to take me to the pastoral offices, where I work every day. There's probably something He wants to reveal to me about my job. *That* must be it!" But the Holy Spirit continued pulling me farther, past the offices, until there was nowhere else to go but outside.

I felt the Lord turn me around and stop me at the front-most doors of the main entrance. I stood there and stared at the glass doors confused for a second when suddenly I felt my knees give out and my body go limp. I felt a heavy weight of God's glory fall on me. I collapsed to the ground and could not get up as much as I tried, immediately overwhelmed by God's presence. I could feel the power of God within me, surrounding me, and covering me like a full-body glove. Facedown on the ground, I began to weep, undone because I knew I was in the company of the Almighty. My spirit and body were utterly submitted to the Lord, yet my mind was fully aware and filled with questions.

A struggle existed within me. I felt God, but at the same time, I felt my flesh, my logic, and my reasoning wrestle against what He was trying to show me. Instead of staying there and patiently letting God speak to me in His own time, I started giving in to my haste to get up. I thought, "What if someone sees me here on the ground? What if, instead, someone comes through the door and doesn't see me and steps on me? I've got to get up!" More than anything I was self-conscious that someone would see me— the pastor's brother's wife—on the ground and think I'd lost my mind. I'd come a long way from my prideful days, but evidently there was still some pride left to surrender. Needless to say, God was not done with me.

Trying to end the awkwardness of the moment, I fought God's presence. I tried to reach up and grab the door handle to pull myself up. But the attempt was futile. All I was able to do was reach up and place the palm of my hand on the bottom of that door. I had only touched the door when something extraordinary and unbeknownst to me happened. I felt something like an electric current shoot through my hand. As a child I'd accidentally touched rogue currents, so I knew what an electric shock was and how it jerked all my muscles violently. But this was a different kind of current; more than just shaking my body, this one violently quaked on a much deeper level, right through my spirit.

As the shock waves rushed through me, I began to see a vision unlike anything I had seen before. I saw faces, hundreds of thousands of them, flashing before my eyes in what seemed like milliseconds, so fast I couldn't stop to fix my eyes on any of them. I saw people from all over the world, representing every ethnicity, language, age group, and social status. They were all so diverse and different from one another, except for the expression they all shared in common, a wretchedness that came through their eyes; they were lost and in need of a Savior.

Upon seeing this, I was overtaken with a deep despair for these people, whom I did not know and had never thought of before. Such was this despair that an uncontainable heartbreak overtook me, and I began to wail, almost grief-stricken for all these people. My chest felt burdened with a profound aching, and I couldn't breathe. Everything hurt, from my body to the core of my spirit.

"Who are all these people, and why do I feel this hurt inside for people I don't even know?" I thought. I had already learned that when receiving such a poignant message from God, it's important that I push for details and ask the Lord exactly what He's telling me, so I did just that. I addressed my questions—even some frustration—to God and silently prayed to Him, "What is going on, Lord? I don't get what You're trying to tell me! First You take me by the hand and pull me away from the sanctuary, away from the altar, where I thought I belonged. Then You pass me right by the office where I work for You daily, only to bring me to this door, shove my face to the ground, and nearly electrocute me, and now I'm sobbing uncontrollably for all these people I don't even know! What kind of purpose is this that You are trying to show me? What are You trying to tell me?"

Immediately He replied to all my questions and my whining.

I audibly heard Him cry out to me with a desperate scream that shook my entire being: "Go get them! Go get my babies! They're lost and all alone in a terrible world! They can't find their way if no one shows them. I *need* my babies back home with me. GO GET MY BABIES!"

Then and there, lying facedown on the ground with my hand on that door, unable to move, wailing, I understood Him. For a long season I had grown weary of leaving home to go minister through music and preaching. I had been considering no longer doing ministry outside of the four walls of the church because it was the place where I felt safe, stable, and comfortable. Life on the road was unpredictable and exhausting. I questioned whether continuing in this type of ministry was worth leaving my home behind. This experience was exactly what I needed in order to know where my true purpose was: in helping to save God's lost babies.

When I heard His voice scream in such despair, I couldn't help but liken it to that same desperate tone in the voice of every mother who's ever lost a child. The urgency to go find the child in harm's way came clearly to my heart. I understood then that God was downloading these people and their need for Him on to my spirit. Much like when a parent staples a sign of her lost child on every post, the Holy Spirit was imprinting "signs" on my heart. That's why I felt such sorrow and despair for these lost souls; it's almost as if God had allowed my heart to break for what breaks His: rescuing His children.

That day I repented of my self-centered way of thinking. I finally denied myself completely and surrendered whatever was left of my pride at the feet of Jesus. I vowed to follow the cause of Christ, come what may. Through God's supernatural touch I was able to share His heart and realize how important every soul is to Him. Since then I've committed to giving my life, my energy, my gifts and talents, my resources, and whatever influence I have to be a beacon of hope and point the lost in the direction of the cross,

that they too could find Him as I did. I want with all my heart
to carry Christ's burden for the lost and live my best to be God's
hands and feet on earth for as long as I live.

———— ◆ ————

OUR TRUE CALLING

After that amazing experience with God I know that in everything I do my priority must be to follow God's will and make a
way for souls to encounter Him. I've been immensely privileged
to serve God in full-time itinerant ministry. Through the years,
though, I've had to learn quite a bit about what true calling and
ministry are.

The word *ministry* is heard often among Christians when referring to people who do work for God. For instance, when someone
pastors a church organization, it is normal to hear that they lead
a pastoral or church ministry. Those who go around preaching
and inviting people to receive Jesus as Savior are usually known
to have an evangelistic ministry. Additionally the labors of others
who devote themselves to building, caring for, and offering covering to other churches in different regions are typically identified
as having an apostolic ministry. Most people say those who make
music to glorify God are engaged in music ministry. All these are
mere examples of what we call ministries. Yet what is the true
meaning of ministry?

In the past I'd gathered a few impressions of what it was to
be in ministry. The closer I came to it, the clearer my perspective became. At first I had been under the impression that a
person in ministry held a position that was favored above others.
I thought ministry was only a privilege for a select "chosen" few. I
thought of a minister as a strong leader, ordained to hold a high,
unreachable, even untouchable place within the Church of Christ.
Furthermore I did not consider myself to be a minister at all. My
thinking could not have been further from the truth. As I came

closer to the truth, my paradigms began to shift, and my heart aligned with what ministry *really* is and what it is not.

Ministry is not a position, though it may sometimes require that we hold one or even change from one to another; ministry is not a job, though it may require us to do work; ministry is not a privileged status for an elite few, though it most certainly is a privilege that garners the favor of God. To know what ministry truly is, we must start by understanding the meaning of the word itself.

The word *ministry* is basically a synonym of the word *service*.[2] In other words, to minister is to serve. Personally when I understood this simple but profound definition, I could see what ministry is really all about. The best example of it was Jesus. Mark 10:45 says, "For even the Son of Man did not come to be served, but to serve, and to give His life a ransom for many."

> Ministry is not a position, though it may sometimes require that we hold one or even change from one to another; ministry is not a job, though it may require us to do work; ministry is not a privileged status for an elite few, though it most certainly is a privilege that garners the favor of God.

The word *serve* in that verse comes from the Greek root word *diakonéō* (pronounced dee-ak-on-eh'-o), which means to wait at a table, particularly a slave who waits on guests. It also means to actively serve, as one who is constantly kicking up dirt from being so active from one place to another in service. Additionally Strong's Concordance defines it as "caring for the needs of others as the Lord guides in an *active, practical* way."[3] Interestingly this word is also interchangeable with the word *minister*, as we see in Young's Literal Translation of the Bible, which says, "for even the Son of Man came not to be *ministered to*, but to *minister*, and to give his life a ransom for many" (Mark 10:45, emphasis added).

As we can see here, ministry and service are one and the same. But this kind of service is not a partial or limited kind but an intentional and active kind. Ministry is to dedicate our lives as

Jesus did, surrendering ourselves to follow God and His will and to save others. It is not reserved for those who choose it as a vocation; it is an attitude of service and a decision to do everything you do as unto God and for the sake of bringing hope. Whether we work in vocational ministry or in secular positions, as believers our true calling in all we do is to serve God, serve His people, and save the lost.

WANTING WHAT GOD WANTS

To best serve God, we have to know what He wants. But what does God want? Have you ever wondered what the greatest desire of His heart is? I sure have, many times. In fact, realizing and following God's desire have become the center of my existence. And the more I discover of Him, the more awestruck I am of His greatness and the more I hunger for His presence.

In my pursuit of God's heart, I've sought out ways to better relate to Him in order to know Him more. Since God is a person—He has a personality, feelings, and desires—I can identify with Him as such. Usually a person's thoughts are driven by his or her desires. Jeremiah 29:11 perfectly summarizes God's thoughts for His children: "For I know the thoughts that I think toward you, says the LORD, thoughts of peace and not of evil, to give you a future and a hope."

God thinks toward us according to what He wants for us: peace and not evil, a future and a hope. For this He has drawn out a plan. The Bible encompasses the story of God's plan and intentions for mankind. As with any good story, the best place to find the end of the story is in the final pages of the book. It is also true with the Bible. The endgame of God's plan can be found in the Book of Revelation, which contains the prophecies of the end of time, given to the apostle John. Revelation 21:1–4 (emphasis added) clearly shows what God's ultimate desire is for us:

Now I saw a new heaven and a new earth, for the first heaven and the first earth had passed away. Also there was no more sea. Then I, John, saw the holy city, New Jerusalem, coming down out of heaven from God, prepared as a bride adorned for her husband. And I heard a loud voice from heaven saying, "Behold, the tabernacle of God is with men, and *He will dwell with them, and they shall be His people.* God Himself will be with them and be their God. And God will *wipe away every tear from their eyes; there shall be no more death, nor sorrow, nor crying. There shall be no more pain, for the former things have passed away.*"

This passage always fills my heart with the hope that awaits the children of God when all is said and done and we are all united with Him in eternity. But to get to this end, there had to be a beginning. This too clearly foreshadows God's ultimate desire. Genesis 1:26–27 (emphasis added) says:

Then God said, "*Let Us make man in Our image, according to Our likeness*; let them have dominion over the fish of the sea, over the birds of the air, and over the cattle, over all the earth and over every creeping thing that creeps on the earth." So God created man in His own image; in the image of God He created him; male and female He created them.

Later in Genesis we see how man, Adam, took charge over the earth but soon became lonely. He desired another like him to be his companion. Remember, God made man in His image and likeness. Then man, whom God made like Himself—from his physical aspects to his emotional tendencies—desired someone like himself to be in relationship with. So God made us like Him, and we want companionship and relationship; therefore that is what God wants also.

Taking Genesis and Revelation together, it is clear to see what God's greatest desire is: He wants *us*! God's initial desire was *us*, and His ending desire is to dwell with *us*, that we would be *His* and He would be *ours*, making our worldly sufferings a thing of the past as we enjoy a perfect relationship and future with Him forever. Hallelujah!

Now, there is more to it than that. As we all know, we are still in this physical world, bound by time and space, which keeps us from enjoying the fullness of our eternity with God. In plain terms since we're not in heaven yet, we are still subject to a continuous battle with sin. Though it is true that God's goal for humanity is for us to be together eternally, this is just the beginning of understanding what God wants of us *now*. This brings us to our current and immediate part in God's grand plan: the Great Commission. Matthew 28:18–20 (emphasis added) says:

> And Jesus came and spoke to them, saying, "All authority has been given to Me in heaven and on earth. *Go therefore and make disciples* of all the nations, *baptizing them* in the name of the Father and of the Son and of the Holy Spirit, *teaching them to observe all things that I have commanded you*; and lo, I am with you always, even to the end of the age." Amen.

Jesus is the key to our salvation. God came to earth through Christ. He lived like a man. He shed His blood and died, paying the ransom for our sin and removing the obstruction that satan put in our way so we wouldn't be able to reach God. Satan's desire has always been to defy God and ruin His plan by leading the world astray (Rev. 12:9, NIV). As the body of Christ we are to be aids in the realization of His plan. We must reach out to those who don't know God and help them find their way back to Him.

We come from God and are meant to return to Him (Rom. 11:36; 1 Cor. 8:6). We were designed with a void inside that can only be filled by God, who has placed an eternal longing in our hearts (Eccles. 3:11). In the same way, He has a longing for us. The heart of God beats for souls. We are the center of His focus since the foundation of the world (Eph. 1:4), He chose us before we chose Him (John 15:16), and He loved us before we loved Him (1 John 4:19). He stopped at nothing to rescue us from our sin through Christ, as John 3:16 says: "For God so loved the world that He gave His only begotten Son, that whoever believes in Him should not perish but have everlasting life."

DOERS, NOT HEARERS ONLY

> When we make our desire the same as God's, and we focus on souls, He will certainly bless our endeavors because it advances His endgame.

Now that we have knowledge of ministry and service, God and His desire for us, and humanity's deep need for Him, what then shall we do with it? Our part is to be Jesus's hands and feet in active support of God's plan. God wants us; He longs deeply for souls. Therefore, we must be intentional in putting to action what we've learned of God's plan. We cannot wholly fulfill our purpose if we do not actively pursue God's desire for souls.

My brother-in-law, Pastor Tito Caban, taught me something that has stuck with me ever since I took my first steps into ministry. He said, "In whatever you do, remember to keep souls at the forefront of your focus, and you'll surely succeed." Through the years in every project I embark on, I've kept that principle, and the Lord has blessed it. Why? It's simple. When we make our desire the same as God's, and we focus on souls, He will certainly bless our endeavors because it advances His endgame. In other words, if we do what we do to bless people and bring them closer to God, He is compelled to make it work. And He does!

Matthew 6:19–20 says, "Do not lay up for yourselves treasures on earth, where moth and rust destroy and where thieves break in and steal; but lay up for yourselves treasures in heaven, where neither moth nor rust destroys and where thieves do not break in and steal." God's greatest treasure is souls. Therefore they are the best treasure we can lay up in heaven. As we focus on eternal reward over earthly reward, we can rest assured that God's blessing will remain upon us.

However, I know this is easier said than done. There is a sacrifice of self that must take place to follow through with this part of God's plan. For this reason I propose to you, start with small steps. Train your mind to think about what God desires: you and everyone around you. Start by maintaining as a priority blessing someone, at least one person, each day through what you do. If you're in a workplace, for instance, bless someone with a smile and a good attitude. If someone has a need that you can fulfill, don't hesitate to do so as the Lord guides you. If someone needs your prayer, reach out and pray for that person. The most important thing to remember is to not just listen to this but to act on it, even if it requires a little denying of yourself. After all, Jesus did it for us, and we must help others enjoy that privilege too. James chapter 1 says it perfectly:

> Therefore lay aside all filthiness and overflow of wickedness, and receive with meekness the implanted word, which is able to save your souls. But *be doers of the word, and not hearers only*, deceiving yourselves. For if anyone is a hearer of the word and not a doer, he is like a man observing his natural face in a mirror; for he observes himself, goes away, and immediately forgets what kind of man he was. But he who looks into the perfect law of liberty and continues in it, and is *not a forgetful hearer but a doer* of the work, *this one will be blessed in what he does.*
> —JAMES 1:21–25, EMPHASIS ADDED

We are God's desire. His plan is for us to be with Him. But how can the lost know of Christ if no one reaches out to tell them? The Word says the feet of those who go after the lost are "beautiful" (Rom. 10:15; see also vv. 14, 16). Our ministry and greatest calling is to serve God by serving His people. There is no better way to do this than by leading others closer to God through all we do. Even if it means making sacrifices, we can rest assured there will be an eternal reward in heaven for us (Matt. 16:27). So I encourage you to be one of the rescuers of God's babies. Let's bring His lost children home so we can all be together, fulfilling God's greatest dream to spend eternity with us.

PRAYER TO FOLLOW GOD'S PLAN TO REACH OTHERS

Wherever you are in your journey with God, know that His end goal is for us to be with Him forever. Therefore we must intentionally do our part in forwarding the good news of salvation to as many people as we can. There are many ways to reach the lost. Some people are called to vocational ministry, while others' ministry is found within regular, day-to-day activities. Whatever your case may be, know that God is pleased with and blesses those who strive to serve Him in reaching out to others. I encourage you to take hold of the Great Commission, join with Christ in bringing others closer to Him, and pray this prayer:

Dear Lord,

I yearn to want the things You want. I now know that the greatest desire of Your heart is to be with us, Your sons and daughters. Help me be proactive in working toward bringing others closer to You. Grant me the opportunities to share my faith without fear. Give me Your heart for the lost, that You might reach them through my obedience. Strengthen my faith, and teach me how to be a good servant to You and Your people.

In the name of Jesus, by whom we are saved, amen.

SCRIPTURES TO HOLD ON TO

Let your light so shine before men that they may see your good works and glorify your Father who is in heaven.

—MATTHEW 5:16, MEV

For whoever does the will of My Father who is in heaven is My brother, and sister, and mother.

—MATTHEW 12:50, MEV

To him who overcomes I will grant to sit with Me on My throne, as I also overcame and sat down with My Father on His throne.

—REVELATION 3:21

Part V

---•---

~ PRODIGAL ~
HEART

Chapter 12

∾ FOREVER A PRODIGAL ∾

*You will not stroll into Christlikeness with your hands
in your pockets, shoving the door open with a careless
shoulder. This is no hobby for one's leisure moments,
taken up at intervals when we have nothing much to do,
and put down and forgotten when our life grows full and
interesting. . . . It takes all one's strength, and all one's
heart, and all one's mind, and all one's soul, given freely
and recklessly and without restraint.*[1]

—A. J. GOSSIP (1873–1954)
SCOTTISH AUTHOR, THEOLOGIAN,
TEACHER, AND CHURCH LEADER

THIS CHAPTER IS different from all the others. It does
not start with a novelistic description of part of my story.
Neither is it a denouement that seeks to give you a reso-
lution to my story. Why? My story has not ended—and neither
has yours. It won't be until our last breaths on this earth that we
can call our stories finished. Until the day when my life on earth
comes to an end, there are more adventures to be lived and more
wonderful discoveries to be made on my journey with the Father.
Above them all I look forward to many more opportunities to rise
up and live as the child of God I was created to be. And there is
most definitely more tailoring to be done to this *prodigal heart*.

If you're like me, you probably relate those words to the parable
of the prodigal son, found in Luke 15. Perhaps you're as fond of
that story—and Jesus's marvelous storytelling—as I am. Maybe

that's even why you picked up this book. Let's take a closer look at that amazing story in Luke 15:11–24 (emphasis added):

> A certain man had two sons. And the younger of them [inappropriately] said to his father, "Father, give me the portion of goods that falls to me." So he divided to them his livelihood (estate). And not many days after, the younger son gathered [everything he had], journeyed to a far country, and there wasted his possessions with *prodigal* living. But when he had spent all, there arose a severe famine in that land, and he began to [be in need]. Then he went and joined himself to a citizen of that country, and he sent him into his fields to feed swine. He [was so hungry that he] would gladly have filled his stomach with the [carob] pods that the swine ate, [but they could not satisfy his hunger,] and no one gave him anything.
>
> But when he [finally] came to himself, he said, "How many of my father's hired servants have [food] enough and to spare, and I perish with hunger! I will arise and go to my father, and will say to him, 'Father, I have sinned against heaven and before you, and I am no longer worthy to be called your son. Make me like one of your hired servants.'"
>
> And he arose and came to his father. But *when he was still a great way off, his father saw him and had compassion, and ran and fell on his neck and kissed him.* And the son said to him, "Father, I have sinned against heaven and in your sight, and am no longer worthy to be called your son."
>
> But the father said to his servants, "[Quickly] bring out *the best robe* [for the guest of honor] and put it on him, and put *a ring* on his hand and *sandals* on his feet. And bring *the fatted calf* here and kill it, and let us [invite everyone and] *eat and be merry; for this my son was* [as good as] *dead and is alive again; he was lost and is found.*" And they began to be merry.

WHAT IS PRODIGAL?

In this marvelous account of a father's unconditional love, I would like to shed light on some key points. But before we get to those details, we must focus on the meaning of the word *prodigal*, mentioned in verse 13. Many of us have been under the misconception that *prodigal* means lost. However, the true meaning is quite different, in fact.

The dictionary defines *prodigal* as lavishly abundant, profuse, or extravagant.[2] Additionally I like how Pastor Robert Morris describes the word. In his message "Lost and Found" he says, "The definition of *prodigal* is *lacking restraint*. What this means is that all of us are prodigal at some time, in some area of our lives; all of us have been [prodigal] at some point, and maybe even right now."[3]

In combining the two descriptions, we can define *prodigal* as "a person who does not restrain in giving and does so profusely, extravagantly, and with lavish abundance." Whoa. That does not mean lost at all! To me this is a better description of God than it is of any of His children. After all, it was God who gave so abundantly, not withholding even the life of His only Son, Jesus Christ, to save us. From the beginning of time He's held nothing back in an effort to reach us. He's the perfect example of what lack of restraint is, and unrestrained love at that. He's stopped at nothing to fulfill His greatest desire, which is to be with us forever. In light of this, the story of the prodigal son could have even been better named "The Prodigal Father."

> Many of us have been under the misconception that prodigal means lost.

Therefore, I propose, if *prodigal* is lacking restraint, and if our best example of this is our heavenly Father, who gave it all for us, shouldn't we reciprocate that unrestrained love toward Him and His people? I certainly do believe that we *should* and we *must*. You see, we were nothing; we were lost in our sin, swaying in different directions, without a clear path to follow, until the lavishly profuse and extravagant love of God found us. Had it not been for Someone—the greatest of "someones"—unleashing all His intentions, efforts, resources, and energy to find us, we'd still be lost, perhaps forever. It is precisely because of God's prodigal love for us that we must live prodigally, not for ourselves, but for Him.

OBTAINING A PRODIGAL HEART

You may be asking yourself, "What is a prodigal heart?," or "How can I have one?" A prodigal heart is nothing other than one who lives unrestrained for the glory of God and the service of God's people. It is someone who holds nothing back from loving and pleasing the Lord, someone who stops at nothing to give the lost a chance to find Jesus and be saved—even if it involves denying himself to be an example of God's love. A prodigal heart is one who chooses to willfully give up his life and earthly desires every day for the sake of following God's will and not his own. Finally a prodigal heart maintains his focus on eternity and the things that are higher than the finite nature of this earth—his feet on the ground and his mind on heaven—knowing that earthly reward is nothing compared with the treasure we can store up in heaven if we live for God and not ourselves.

> We were nothing; we were lost in our sin, swaying in different directions, without a clear path to follow, until the lavishly profuse and extravagant love of God found us.

Developing a prodigal heart is both easy and difficult. It is easy because it's simple. The only requirement for it is to love God with everything or, as Jesus said in Mark 12:30–31 (AMP), "And you shall *love* the Lord your God with all your heart, and with all your soul (life), and with all your mind (thought, understanding), and with all your strength.' This is the second: 'You shall [unselfishly] *love* your neighbor as yourself.' There is no other commandment greater than these" (emphasis added). To truly understand the profound simplicity of this statement, it is important to know that both occurrences of the word *love* in this passage come from the Greek word *agape*, which, more than reflecting the emotion of love, refers to doing things for the benefit of someone else, having unselfish concern for another person and a willingness to seek her best interest.[4] Therefore the easy part in having a prodigal heart for God is loving Him with everything and loving people as you love yourself, thus having an unselfish concern for their well-being and doing things to benefit them.

The difficult part of living prodigally for God is that to do so, you must deny yourself and your own desires. Jesus said in Luke 9:23, "*If anyone wishes to follow Me* [as My disciple], *he must deny himself* [set aside selfish interests], and *take up his cross daily* [expressing a willingness to endure whatever may come] *and follow Me* [believing in Me, conforming to My example in living and, if need be, suffering or perhaps dying because of faith in Me]" (AMP, emphasis added). To be prodigal, as Jesus was, we must deny ourselves. Why? The reason is our flesh often gets in the way of what our spirit—what joins us to the Father—wants (Gal. 5:17).

A life of self-denial for God does indeed have its fair share of challenges and afflictions. In John 16:33 Jesus said: "I have told you these things, so that in Me you may have [perfect] peace. In the world you have tribulation and distress and suffering, but be courageous [be confident, be undaunted, be filled with joy]; I have overcome the world. [My conquest is accomplished, My victory abiding]" (AMP). We have a profound and enduring hope in Christ Jesus, who has overcome all the challenges we may face in this world. We can rest assured that, though we may suffer for His cause while on this earth, by Him we are assured that when all has passed, we shall have a place with Him beside the Father. Denying ourselves in this world is nothing but a test of endurance—and a very short one compared with the rest of eternity.

For instance, to truly fulfill the calling God placed before me, I had to give up my desires for fame and fortune, not because they were bad things but because they would have certainly fed my ego and pride. This would have undoubtedly caused me to drift away from God and His purpose in me—as it had already begun to do when God rescued me. Had I disobeyed God instead of surrendering to His love, His plan for my life—to reach the lost and be an example of redemption and God's miraculous restoration—would have been tampered with. Had I not denied myself and allowed my love for God to be bigger than anything in my life, I'm certain I would not have witnessed the salvation and transformation of thousands of people around the world in His name. And I likely would not have written this book.

> One thing is for sure: you are a prodigal—lacking restraint—in something. It's time to be prodigal for the One who recklessly abandoned and poured out the most prodigal love for you.

Yes, I did leave it all behind for the cause of Christ. Am I glad I did? You bet! I've seen every one of God's promises come to fulfillment. I've experienced His faithfulness firsthand in providing every one of my needs. More so, I've learned that a life of dependence on God is the best kind. Now that I know how certain and constant God's love, mercy, grace, and faithfulness are, I can understand that He was always right to ask me to take the leap of faith and follow Him above all else. Living through the adventures of faith with Jesus is an absolute highlight of my life; just the thought of resorting back to when I was in control of my life now seems like the greatest of absurdities.

I am a prodigal heart because I was created for it. And so were you! It doesn't matter where you've been, what you've done, or even if where you're standing in life right now seems to disqualify you from being all God wants you to be. One thing is for sure: you are a prodigal—lacking restraint—in something. It's time to be prodigal for the One who recklessly abandoned and poured out the most prodigal love for you. So love God, follow God, serve God, and with your life make way for others to do the same. Let your prodigal heart beat to the rhythm of God's.

PRAY OVER YOUR PRODIGAL HEART

While living for God is marvelous, it is not void of challenges. One of the greatest of these challenges is wrestling with our own humanity, which continually pulls us away from God. The greatest weapons against the adverse forces that intend to pry us away from the Father are self-denial, resistance, and prayer. Therefore I encourage you to take up your cross, follow Christ, and live out loud for His sake, holding nothing back.

If you are ready to let your prodigal heart beat for God above all else, pray this prayer:

> *Dear God,*
>
> *You are a prodigal God; You gave it all for me just to express Your love and interest for me. I've realized that I have been prodigal for the wrong things in life. But today I declare that this changes. I now understand that the full life You promise is not one that clamps us down but one that allows us to release the fullness of Your love in us. Help me be the prodigal heart that You desire. Show me how to lack restraint in my love, pursuit, and service for You, Your kingdom, and Your people. From this moment on and in Your name I am unleashed and freed to live prodigally for You and not myself.*
>
> *In Jesus's name, it is done, amen.*

SCRIPTURES TO HOLD ON TO

Let your light so shine before men that they may see your good works and glorify your Father who is in heaven.
—MATTHEW 5:16, MEV

Then he said to the crowd, "If any of you wants to be my follower, you must give up your own way, take up your cross daily, and follow me."
—LUKE 9:23, NLT

I have told you all this so that you may have peace in me. Here on earth you will have many trials and sorrows. But take heart, because I have overcome the world.

—John 16:33, NLT

Blessed is the man who endures temptation; for when he has been approved, he will receive the crown of life which the Lord has promised to those who love Him.

—James 1:12

Be faithful until death, and I will give you the crown of life.

—Revelation 2:10

...not my will, but yours be done.

—Luke 22:42, NIV

Afterword

❧ COME TO JESUS ❧

I WOULD LIKE TO end these pages with an opportunity—the best anyone can ever be offered. This is for the people who were touched by the message shared in this book, the ones who felt a resonance deep within them, a call from God to open their hearts to Him. If you've realized you do not yet know God, I would like to offer you an invitation to welcome Him into your heart and give your heart to Jesus, who already gave His life as a sacrifice for your sin.

Maybe you've never asked God into your heart or acknowledged Him as your one and true Savior. Or perhaps you have done this in the past, but because of decisions you've made, you are no longer in a good-standing relationship with God. Whatever your case may be, if you are not certain you are saved, and if you haven't surrendered your life to the God who loves you and paid the ultimate price as a ransom for your life, I invite you to accept Jesus as your Savior and invite Him into your heart.

Following I offer a prayer to help you do this. But please know the prayer is just a guide for you. It is not part of a "formula" to be saved, as there is no such thing other than coming to God with honesty, humility, surrender, and repentance. It is absolutely all right for you to use your own words to express your desire to God and your need for salvation. If you'd like to do that, I encourage you to pray something like this:

> *Dear Lord Jesus,*
> *Thank You for appointing this day as the day of my sal-*
> *vation. I confess that I have sinned in more ways than I*

can count or describe. As the prodigal son with his father, I know that because of my sin I do not deserve to be called Your child. I am a sinner in need of a savior.

I acknowledge that I have heard of You, Jesus, who being God came to earth, lived like a man, died a horrendous death on the cross, shed Your blood for me, and rose again on the third day just to save me. Please wash away my sins, as I freely receive Your precious blood and sacrifice. Cleanse me from my past, renew me with Your love, and restore me with Your grace.

From this day forward I declare that You, Jesus Christ, are my only Lord and Savior. I surrender my life to You and give You my heart. From now on I promise to love You, pursue You, and serve You until the day when we meet face-to-face. Write my name in Your book of life, and let my life be the reward for Your suffering on the cross of Calvary.

I welcome You, Holy Spirit, into my life and submit to Your will and guidance. God, today I accept You. Your love now casts out any darkness in me and brings forth Your wonderful light in my life.

Today I am saved and freed from my sin by the power of Your love and by my faith in You, Jesus Christ. Amen.

NOW WHAT?

If you have said this prayer and received Jesus into your heart, I want to congratulate you for making the best decision you could ever make, one that you will carry into eternity. You have now passed from death to life. Here is a perfect depiction of what you have just done:

> And you He made alive, who were dead in trespasses and sins, in which you once walked according to the course of this world, according to the prince of the power of the air, the spirit who now works in the sons of disobedience, among whom also we all once conducted ourselves in the lusts of our flesh, fulfilling the desires of the flesh and of

the mind, and were by nature children of wrath, just as the others.

But God, who is rich in mercy, *because of His great love with which He loved us,* even when we were dead in trespasses, *made us alive together with Christ* (by grace you have been saved), and raised us up together, and made us sit together in the heavenly places in Christ Jesus, *that in the ages to come He might show the exceeding riches of His grace in His kindness toward us in Christ Jesus. For by grace you have been saved through faith,* and that not of yourselves; it is the gift of God, not of works, lest anyone should boast. For we are His workmanship, created in Christ Jesus for good works, which God prepared beforehand that we should walk in them.

—EPHESIANS 2:1–10, EMPHASIS ADDED

You are now made new by God,, as 2 Corinthians 5:17 says: "Therefore, if anyone is in Christ, he is a new creation; old things have passed away; behold, *all things have become new*" (emphasis added). To now live your life according to God's will, you must keep a few simple things in mind on your journey of faith with God.

Pray every day.

Praying is nothing other than talking with God and listening to Him. There is not a formal format you need to follow to pray. Simply talk with God throughout your day every day, as you would with your best friend, which is now the Holy Spirit. Tell Him about your feelings, your needs, your hurts, your joys, your dreams, your aspirations, and whatever you may need help with. The Bible says prayer can benefit very much, to the point of healing the sick and delivering people from inner wounds and sin (James 5:15–16). So every day talk to God, pray.

Read the Bible.

I like to call the Bible the most amazing love letter ever written; it is *God's* love letter to His children. Some people say "BIBLE" is an acronym for "basic instructions before leaving earth."[1] The answer to every relevant question in life is found in the Scriptures. The more we study them, the more revelation and wisdom we receive from God and the closer we draw to Him. Read the Bible every day, and you'll see how much your spiritual life grows!

Join a church family.

I know this may be a touchy subject, possibly because of having a not-so-good experience with a hyper-religious churchgoer. I can personally relate to that, and I understand it well. There is one thing you should know, though: when Jesus said in the world we would have afflictions (John 16:33), He also referred to being hurt by other people. In other words, where there is another human being, there will always be a chance that person will hurt, fail, or disappoint you. However, as you've just invited the Holy Spirit into your heart, you can be sure that He is now your very best Friend, and He will never hurt you or fail you or lie to you; He will lead you to all truth (John 16:13)!

It is important to find a church family that truly preaches the Word of God. God places the lonely in families where they can help one another heal and be set free (Ps. 68:6), for where two or three are gathered in His name, there He is among them (Matt. 18:20). As with any family, some are strong when others are weak. One carries the burdens of another as they take turns being strong for each other in Christ's name (Gal. 6:2). Furthermore, it is a place where the children of God are known for the love they have for one another (John 13:35). Find a place where the Word of God is true and unaltered, where people love people, and where you can grow spiritually with the help of others.

Life ahead of you is wonderful! Make sure to keep Jesus at the center of your life, talk with God every day, read His Word, and join a faith group where you can grow and live out the fullness of your purpose in Christ. I am praying for you. Let your *prodigal heart* beat on for God!

∾ NOTES ∾

Introduction
1. Timothy Keller, *The Prodigal God: Recovering the Heart of the Christian Faith* (London: Penguin Books, 2008), 2. Kindle edition.
2. *Baker's Evangelical Dictionary of Biblical Theology*, s.v. "Satan," accessed April 17, 2017, http://www.biblestudytools.com /dictionaries/bakers-evangelical-dictionary/satan.html.

Chapter 1: The Setting
1. "Facts for Families No. 1: Children and Divorce," American Academy of Child and Adolescent Psychiatry, March 2011, accessed April 19, 2017, http://www.aacap.org/AACAP/Families_and_Youth /Facts_for_Families/Facts_for_Families_Pages/Children_and _Divorce_01.aspx.
2. "Child Abuse Facts," Compassion International, accessed April 19, 2017, http://www.compassion.com/poverty/child-abuse.htm.
3. World Health Organization, *World Report on Violence and Health*, page 149, accessed April 19, 2017, http://www.who.int/violence _injury_prevention/violence/global_campaign/en/chap6.pdf.
4. "Child Trafficking Statistics," Ark of Hope for Children, updated March 19, 2016, accessed April 19, 2017, http://arkofhopefor children.org/child-trafficking/child-trafficking-statistics.
5. "What Is Child Abuse?," Child Abuse, accessed April 19, 2017, https://sites.google.com/site/childabuse111/1.
6. Ibid.
7. Ibid.
8. *Merriam-Webster's Collegiate Dictionary*, eleventh edition (Springfield, MA: Merriam-Webster Inc., 2003), s.v. "setting."
9. WordReference.com, s.v. "set," accessed April 20, 2017, http://www .wordreference.com/definition/set.

Chapter 2: Loss, Pain, and Grief

1. "A. J. Gossip Quotes," oChristian.com, accessed April 20, 2017, http://christian-quotes.ochristian.com/A.J.-Gossip-Quotes/.
2. WordReference.com, s.v. "grieve," accessed April 20, 2017, http://www.wordreference.com/definition/grieve.
3. "Men Crying in the Bible," Net-burst.net, accessed April 21, 2017, http://www.net-burst.net/hope/weeping.htm.
4. "Living Through Grief," CBN.com, accessed April 21, 2017, http://www.cbn.com/spirituallife/CBNTeachingSheets/Grief.aspx.
5. Ibid.
6. Mary M. Lyles, "Children's Grief Responses," 2010, accessed April 24, 2017, http://www.childgrief.org/howtohelp.htm#NFANTS.
7. "Grief and Children," American Academy of Child and Adolescent Psychiatry, updated July 2013, accessed April 24, 2017, http://www.aacap.org/AACAP/Families_and_Youth/Facts_for_Families/FFF-Guide/Children-And-Grief-008.aspx.
8. "How to Help Someone Who Is Grieving," Cancer*Care*, accessed April 24, 2017, http://www.cancercare.org/publications/67-how_to_help_someone_who_is_grieving.

Chapter 3: Rejection

1. "Watchman Nee Quotes," oChristian.com, accessed April 25, 2017, http://christian-quotes.ochristian.com/Watchman-Nee-Quotes/page-8.shtml.
2. "Rejection Roots," Gateway Church, September 6, 2014, accessed April 26, 2017, http://gatewaypeople.com/ministries/life/events/room-12/session/2014/09/06/rejection-roots, minute 7:49.
3. "Rejection Roots," Gateway Church, minute 9:47.

Chapter 4: Fear and Doubt

1. "Corrie Ten Boom Quotes," oChristian.com, accessed April 27, 2017, http://christian-quotes.ochristian.com/Corrie-Ten-Boom-Quotes/.
2. WordReference.com, s.v. "fear," accessed April 27, 2017, http://www.wordreference.com/definition/fear.
3. WordReference.com, s.v. "doubt," accessed April 27, 2017, http://www.wordreference.com/definition/doubt.

4. David Ropeik, "EMBO Reports: The Consequences of Fear," US National Library of Medicine, National Institutes of Health, October 5, 2004, accessed April 27, 2017, http://www.ncbi.nlm.nih.gov/pmc/articles/PMC1299209/.
5. Ibid.
6. "30 Days of Thoughts (From *Great Day Every Day*)," Max Lucado, March 22, 2012, accessed April 28, 2017, https://maxlucado.com/30-days-of-thoughts-from-every-day-deserves-a-chance/.
7. *Segen's Medical Dictionary*, s.v. "hematidrosis," accessed April 28, 2017, http://medical-dictionary.thefreedictionary.com/hematidrosis.
8. Joyce Meyer, "What to Do if You're Tired of Toughing It Out," Joyce Meyer Ministries, accessed May 2, 2017, http://www.joycemeyer.org/articles/ea.aspx?article=what_to_do_if_youre_tired_toughing_it_out.

Chapter 5: Rebellion
1. "C. S. Lewis Quotes," oChristian.com, accessed April 25, 2017, http://christian-quotes.ochristian.com/C.S.-Lewis-Quotes/page-7.shtml.
2. "C. S. Lewis Quotes," oChristian.com, accessed April 25, 2017, http://christian-quotes.ochristian.com/C.S.-Lewis-Quotes/page-27.shtml.

Chapter 6: Grace
1. "D. L. Moody Quotes," oChristian.com, accessed May 9, 2017, http://christian-quotes.ochristian.com/D.L.-Moody-Quotes/page-6.shtml.
2. Bible Hub, s.v. "*metanoeó*," accessed May 9, 2017, http://biblehub.com/greek/3340.htm.

Chapter 7: Resisting Temptation
1. "Ed Cole Quotes," oChristian.com, accessed May 9, 2017, http://christian-quotes.ochristian.com/Ed-Cole-Quotes/.

Chapter 8: Restoration and Inner Healing

1. "Theodore Epp Quotes," oChristian.com, accessed May 10, 2017, http://christian-quotes.ochristian.com/Theodore-Epp-Quotes/.
2. "Caroline Leaf Quotes," Goodreads, accessed May 11, 2017, https://www.goodreads.com/author/quotes/773964.Caroline _Leaf.
3. WordReference.com, s.v. "judgment," accessed May 11, 2017, http://www.wordreference.com/definition/judgment.
4. WordReference.com, s.v. "judge," accessed May 11, 2017, http://www.wordreference.com/definition/judge.
5. WordReference.com, s.v. "forgive," accessed May 11, 2017, http://www.wordreference.com/definition/forgiveness.
6. Danielle Bernock, *Emerging With Wings: A True Story of Lies, Pain, and the Love That Heals* (Detroit, MI: 4F Media, 2014), 138.
7. "Joyce Meyer Quotes," oChristian.com, accessed May 12, 2017, http://christian-quotes.ochristian.com/Joyce-Meyer-Quotes.
8. Caroline Leaf, *Switch on Your Brain: The Key to Peak Happiness, Thinking, and Health* (Grand Rapids, MI: Baker Books, 2013), 33.
9. Ibid., 53.
10. Ibid., 55–56.

Chapter 9: He Is My Father

1. "Confessions of Saint Augustine," Christian Classics Ethereal Library, accessed May 12, 2017, https://www.ccel.org/ccel/augustine /confess.iv.vi.html.
2. Bible Hub, s.v. "Abba," accessed May 12, 2017, http://biblehub.com /greek/5.htm.

Chapter 10: I Am His Child

1. Jonathan David and Melissa Helser, "No Longer Slaves," *We Will Not Be Shaken* (Live) (Redding, CA: Bethel Music, 2015). Used with permission.
2. "Max Lucado Quotes," oChristian.com, accessed May 12, 2017, http://christian-quotes.ochristian.com/Max-Lucado-Quotes/page -2.shtml.
3. WordReference.com, s.v. "son," accessed May 14, 2017, http://www .wordreference.com/definition/son.

4. Bob Hamp, *Think Differently, Live Differently: Keys to a Life of Freedom* (Southlake, TX: Thinking Differently Press, 2010), 29–30.

5. Easton's Bible Dictionary, s.v. "Abba," accessed May 15, 2017, http://www.biblestudytools.com/dictionaries/eastons-bible-dictionary/abba.html.

Chapter 11: "Go Get My Babies"

1. "Charles Spurgeon Quotes," oChristian.com, accessed May 15, 2017, http://christian-quotes.ochristian.com/Charles-Spurgeon-Quotes/page-19.shtml.

2. WordReference.com, s.v. "ministry," accessed May 15, 2017, http://www.wordreference.com/synonyms/ministry.

3. Strong's Concordance #1247, s.v. "*diakoneó*," accessed May 15, 2017, http://biblehub.com/greek/1247.htm.

Chapter 12: Forever a Prodigal

1. "A.J. Gossip Quotes," oChristian.com, accessed May 15, 2017, http://christian-quotes.ochristian.com/A.J.-Gossip-Quotes/.

2. WordReference.com, s.v. "prodigal," accessed May 15, 2017, http://www.wordreference.com/definition/prodigal.

3. Robert Morris, *The Way Home* (video of sermon from "Lost and Found" series, Gateway Church, Southlake, Texas), October 10, 2015, accessed May 15, 2017, http://gatewaypeople.com/ministries/life/events/lost-found-a-gateway-series/session/2015/10/10/the-way-home.

4. Bible Gateway, "Mark 12:29-31," accessed May 15, 2017, https://www.biblegateway.com/passage/?search=Mark+12:29-31&version=AMP#en-AMP-24705.

Afterword: Come to Jesus

1. Adam Christing, *Comedy Comes Clean: A Hilarious Collection of Wholesome Jokes, Quotes, and One-Liners* (New York: Three Rivers Press, 1996), 75.

CONNECT WITH US!

CHARISMA HOUSE

(Spiritual Growth)

[f] Facebook.com/CharismaHouse

[y] @CharismaHouse

[o] Instagram.com/CharismaHouse

SILOAM

(Health)

[p] Pinterest.com/CharismaHouse

MODERN
ENGLISH
VERSION

(Bible)
www.mevbible.com